D0661128

Basic Concepts in Kabbalah

Rav Michael Laitman, PhD

Basic Concepts in Kabbalah

LAITMAN
KABBALAH PUBLISHERS

Rav Michael Laitman, PhD

Translation: David Brushin
Proofreading: Josia Nakash, David Robbins,
Susan Morales Kosinec, Rob Taylor, Robert Jochelson
Editors: Claire Gerus, Michael R. Kellogg
Layout and Drawings: Baruch Khovov
Cover Design: Richard Aquan
Printing and Post Porduction: Uri Laitman
Project Coordinator: Leah Goldberg
Executive Editor: Chaim Ratz

Laitman Kabbalah Publishers Website:
www.kabbalah.info
Laitman Kabbalah Publishers E-mail:
info@kabbalah.info

BASIC CONCEPTS
IN KABBALAH

Published by Laitman Kabbalah Publishers
1057 Steeles Avenue West, Suite 532, Toronto, ON, M2R 3X1, Canada
Printed in Canada

ISBN: 0-9738268-8-6
FIRST EDITION: JULY 2006

The Tree of Life

Behold that before the emanations were emanated and the creatures were created,
The upper simple light had filled the whole existence.
And there was no vacancy, such as an empty atmosphere, a hollow, or a pit,
But all was filled with simple, boundless light.
And there was no such part as head, or tail,
But everything was simple, smooth light, balanced evenly and equally,
And it was called the Endless Light.

And when upon His simple will, came the desire to create the world
and emanate the emanations,
To bring to light the perfection of His deeds, His names, His appellations,
Which was the cause of the creation of the worlds,
He then restricted Himself, in the middle,
Precisely in the center,
He restricted the light.
And the light drew far off to the sides around that middle point.
And there remained an empty space, a vacuum
Circling the middle point.
And the restriction had been uniform
Around the empty point,
So that the space
Was evenly circled around it.

There, after the restriction,
Having formed a vacuum and a space
Precisely in the middle of the endless light,
A place was formed,
Where the emanated and the created might reside.
Then from the Endless Light a single line hung down,
Lowered down into that space.
And through that line, He emanated, created, formed, and
Made all the worlds.
Before these four worlds came to be
There was one infinite, one name, in wondrous, hidden unity,
And even In the angles closest to Him
There is no force and no attainment in the endless,
As there is no mind that can perceive Him,
For He has no place, no boundary, no name.

The ARI,
a great 16th century Kabbalist

Basic Concepts
in Kabbalah

TABLE OF CONTENTS

AUTHOR'S NOTE

Even though this book may seem very basic, it is not intended to be a book that conveys basic knowledge of Kabbalah. Rather, it is a book to help readers cultivate an *approach to the concepts* of Kabbalah, to spiritual objects, and to spiritual terms.

By reading and re-reading in this book, one develops internal observations, senses, and approaches that did not previously exist within. These newly acquired observations are like sensors that "feel" the space around us that is hidden from our ordinary senses.

Hence, this book is intended to foster the contemplation of spiritual terms. To the extent that we are integrated with these terms, we can begin to see with our inner vision the unveiling of the spiritual structure that surrounds us, almost as if a mist had been lifted.

Again, this book is not aimed at the study of facts. Instead, it is a book for beginners who wish to awaken the deepest and subtlest sensations they can possess.

Michael Laitman

INTRODUCTION

Open slightly your heart to me,
and I will reveal the world to you.
-The Book of Zohar

- Who am I?

- Why do I exist?

- Where did we come from? Where are we going? And what is our purpose here?

- Have we been in this world before?

- Why is there suffering in this world and can we avoid it?

- How can we attain peace, fulfillment, and happiness?

From generation to generation, people try to find answers to these painfully insistent questions. The fact that they continue from generation to generation indicates that we still have not received satisfactory answers to them.

While studying nature and the universe, we discover that all that surrounds us exists and functions according to precise and purposeful laws. Yet, when we examine ourselves, the zenith of Creation, we find that humanity seemingly exists outside of this system of rational laws.

For example, when we observe how wisely nature created our bodies and how precisely and purposefully every cell in our bodies functions, we are unable to answer the question: "Why does the entire organism exist?"

All that surrounds us is permeated with cause-and-effect connections. Nothing is created without a purpose; the physical world is governed by precise laws of motion, transformation, and circulation. However, the main question—"Why does it all exist (not only us, but the entire universe)?"—remains unanswered. Is there anyone in this world who has not been touched by this question at least once?

The existing scientific theories assert that the world is governed by invariable physical laws that we are unable to influence. Our only task is to live well by using them wisely and to prepare the ground for the future generations. But good living does not resolve the question concerning why these future generations will, or should, exist.

The question of humanity's origins—whether from a primitive species through evolution, or through extraterrestrial visitations and settlement—does not change the essential questions. There are two primary dates in every person's life: birth and death. What happens between them can be unique and therefore priceless. It can also be meaningless if at the end of it is darkness and chasm.

Where is our wise, omniscient, coherent nature that does nothing without purpose? Every atom, every cell in the human organism has its cause and purpose; yet, what is the purpose of the entire organism? Perhaps there exist some laws and goals that we have not yet discovered.

We can research something at a lower evolutionary level than our own. We perceive and comprehend the meaning of inanimate, vegetative, and animate existence. But we cannot comprehend the meaning of human existence. Evidently, this understanding can be attained only from a higher existential level.

Our research of the world boils down to the study of how it reacts to our influence on it. We can only research at our own level and not above it. Even when we research at our own level, we study it by applying some impact on the world and measuring the reaction to the impact. We perceive our influence on the world with our five senses: sight, sound, smell, taste, and touch. Otherwise, we may use instruments that expand the sensitivity range of our limited senses.

Unfortunately, we cannot recognize anything beyond what our senses can perceive and research. It is as though nothing exists but what we perceive. Whatever does seem to exist, lives only in what we sense, and a creature with different senses would experience the same things in a totally different way.

At the same time, we do not feel a lack of sensory organs, such as a sixth finger on our hands. Just as it is impossible to explain the meaning of eyesight to one blind from birth, so, too, will we fail to discover the concealed forms of nature with the research methods we are applying today.

According to Kabbalah, there exists a spiritual world that is imperceptible to our sense organs. At its center is one tiny part—our universe and our planet--the heart of this universe. This sphere of information, thoughts, and emotions affects us through the laws of the material nature and its incidents. It also places us under certain conditions upon which we must act.

We do not choose where, when, with whom, and with what traits and inclinations we will be born. We do not choose whom to meet and in what environment to grow. These things determine all of our actions and reactions, as well as all of their consequences. So where is our freedom of will?

According to Kabbalah, there are four mandatory kinds of knowledge to attain:

Creation: The study of Creation and the evolution of the worlds, namely:

- The way the Creator created the worlds with the creatures that populate them through consecutive restrictions;

- The interaction laws between the spiritual and material worlds, and their consequences;

- The goal of man's creation is to form a system with an illusion of the existence of free will by combining the soul with the body, and by controlling them through nature and the apparent factor of chance with the help of two mutually balanced systems of light and dark forces.

Functioning: The study of the human essence—its interconnection and interaction with the spiritual world. Functioning deals with one's arrival to—and departure from—this world. It also includes the Upper Worlds' reactions to our world and towards other human beings, caused by man's actions. It researches everyone's individual path, from the creation of worlds to the attainment of the ultimate goal.

Incarnations of the Soul: The study of every soul's essence and its incarnations, as well as our actions in this life and their consequences for subsequent lives. The research of incarnations examines how and why a soul descends to a body, and what determines the acceptance of a certain soul within a certain body.

Incarnations of the Soul also deals with the mystery of chance, and researches human history as a result of a certain order and cycles of souls. It also follows this path over 6,000 years and studies the connection of the soul with the general governance of the system of worlds and its cycles of life and death. It also states upon what factors our path in this world depends.

Governance: The study of our world: inanimate, vegetative, and animate levels of nature, their essence, role, and how they are governed by the spiritual world. It studies the Upper Governance and our perception of nature, time, and space. It researches the Upper Forces that move material bodies, and the way one's inner force pushes all things, animate and inanimate, to the preordained goal.

Can one solve this fundamental puzzle of human life without touching upon the question of its source? Every human being encounters this question. The search for the goal and the meaning of existence is the key question around humankind's spiritual life. Hence, starting with the second half of the 20th century, we are observing a revival of mankind's spiritual aspirations.

The technical progress and global catastrophes that gave rise to a variety of philosophies have not brought spiritual fulfillment to humanity. As Kabbalah explains, out of all existing pleasures, our world received only a tiny spark—its presence in corporeal objects is what provides all our worldly pleasures.

In other words, all our pleasant sensations, from whatever source, are caused only by the presence of this spark within them. Throughout our lives, we are placed in a forced quest of new objects of delight, hoping to receive greater and greater pleasures; we do not suspect that they might not be anything but shells.

To receive absolute fulfillment, we must acknowledge the need for spiritual elevation above matter. There are two paths in our world to reach that goal: the path of the spiritual ascent (Kabbalah), and the path of suffering.

The path of Kabbalah is a path of independent and voluntary realization of the need to gradually terminate egoism, when the Upper Light is used to perceive egoism as evil.

Sometimes people come to this realization quite unexpectedly. A secular, well-established, calm person suddenly begins to feel acute discontent; any spark of excitement, joy, taste for living, and pleasure disappears from that person's everyday life.

This is the state of our generation, where material abundance gives rise to a sensation of spiritual hunger. We start searching for other sources of fulfillment, often choosing a long and prickly path. Freedom of will exists between the paths of spiritual ascent and the path of suffering. One can only wish that people will "choose life" instead of embarking on the path of suffering, the same path upon which we so often treaded in the past.

CHAPTER 1
THE METHOD OF PERCEPTION IN KABBALAH

Kabbalah teaches about the cause-and-effect connection between spiritual sources that unite according to absolute laws into one exalted goal: the attainment of the Creator by the created beings existing in this world.

According to Kabbalah, all of humanity and every individual must reach this ultimate point to fully attain the goal and program of Creation. Throughout the generations, individuals have attained a certain spiritual level through individual work. These people, called "Kabbalists," climbed to the top of the spiritual ladder.

Every material object and its action, from the smallest to the greatest, is operated by spiritual forces that fill our entire universe. It is as if our universe were resting on a net of forces.

Take, for example, the tiniest living organism whose role is merely to reproduce and sustain its species. Think about how many forces and complex systems function within it, and how many of them remain undetected by the human eye. If we multiply them by the number of organisms living today, and by those that once lived in our universe and in the spiritual worlds, we will then have a vague idea of the vast number of forces and connections that control them.

One can depict the spiritual forces as two interconnected and equal systems. The difference between them is that one comes from the Creator and develops from up downward through all the worlds to our world. The other begins in our world and rises according to the laws that were developed in the first system and now function in the second.

Kabbalah defines the first system as "The order of creation of worlds and *Sefirot*," and the second as "The attainments or levels of prophecy and spirit." The second system teaches that people who wish to attain the ultimate degree should follow the laws of the first system, which are the laws studied in Kabbalah. When one ascends in these degrees, the second factor is born within. This is spirituality.

The corporeal world is full of forces and phenomena that we do not feel directly, such as electricity and magnetism, but even small children are familiar with their names and the results of their actions. For example, although our knowledge of electricity is limited, we have learned to utilize this phenomenon for our purposes and define it as naturally as we give names to such things as bread and sugar.

Similarly, it is as if all names in Kabbalah give us a real and objective idea about a spiritual object. On second thought, just as we have no idea about spiritual objects or even the Creator Himself, so are we equally ignorant of any objects, even those we can grip with our hands. This is because we perceive not the object itself, but our reaction to its impact on our senses.

These reactions give us the semblance of knowledge, though the essence of the object itself remains totally concealed from us. Moreover, we are utterly unable to understand even ourselves. All that we know about ourselves is limited to our actions and reactions.

As an instrument of the world's research, science divides into two parts: the study of properties of matter and the study of its form. In other words, there is nothing in the universe that does not consist of matter and form. For example, a table is a combination of matter and form, where matter, such as wood, is the basis that carries the form—that of a table. Or take the word, "liar," where matter (one's body) is a carrier of the form, falsehood.

A science that studies materials is based on tests-experiments that lead to scientific conclusions. However, a science that studies forms irrespective of matter, and separates them abstractly, cannot be based on an experiment. This is even truer with forms that were never connected to matter, because a form without matter does not exist in our world.

A form can be separated from matter only in one's imagination. Therefore, all conclusions in such cases will be based purely on theoretical assumptions. All of philosophy refers to this kind of science, and humanity has often suffered from the unsubstantiated conclusions of philosophers. Most modern scientists have rejected this kind of research because its conclusions are completely unreliable.

While researching the spiritual worlds, we discover that our perceptions are merely a will from Above that wants us to feel as if we are a separately existing entity, and not a part of the Creator. The entire surrounding world is actually the result of the influence of spiritual forces on us. This is why the surrounding world is considered a world of illusions.

Let me explain what I mean with an allegory:

"Once upon a time there lived a coachman. He had a pair of horses, a house, and a family. Suddenly, he had a wave of bad luck: his horses died and so did his wife and children, and his house collapsed. Soon enough the coachman died of grief. At the celestial court, it was discussed what could be given to such a tormented soul. Finally, it was decided to let him *feel* as if he were alive, with his family in his house, as if he had good horses, and was happy with his work and life."

These sensations are sometimes perceived in the same way that a dream seems real. Indeed, only our sensations create our pictures of the surrounding world. So how can we tell illusion from reality?

As with all sciences, Kabbalah, too, is divided into the study of matter and the study of form. Nevertheless, it has a remarkable feature and an edge over other sciences: Even the part of it that studies form abstracted from matter is based entirely on experimental control; that is, it is subject to empirical testing!

When a Kabbalist has risen to the spiritual level of the studied object, he or she acquires its qualities and thereby has full insight.

This person can practically operate various forms of matter, even before they manifest in matter, as if observing our illusions from aside!

Just as with any other teaching, Kabbalah uses certain terminology and symbols to describe objects and actions: a spiritual force, a world, or a *Sefira* is called by the name of the worldly object it controls.

Since every material object or force corresponds to the spiritual object or force that controls it, an utterly precise conformity is created between the name taken from the corporeal world and its spiritual root, its source.

Therefore, only a Kabbalist, who clearly knows the correspondence between spiritual forces and material objects, can assign names to spiritual objects. Only one who has attained the spiritual level of an object can see the consequence of its influence in our world.

Kabbalists write books and pass their knowledge to others using the "language of the branches." This language is exceptionally accurate because it is based on the connection between the spiritual root and the corporeal branch. It cannot be altered due to the invariable connection between an object and its spiritual root. At the same time, our earthly language is gradually losing its accuracy because it is connected only to the branch and not to the root.

However, mere nominal knowledge of the language is insufficient because simply knowing the name of a material object provides no understanding of its spiritual form. Only the knowledge of the spiritual form enables one to see its material result, its branch.

We can thus conclude that one should first attain the spiritual root, its nature and properties. Only then can one pass the name on to its branch in this world and study the interconnection between the spiritual root and the material branch. Only then can one understand the "language of the branches," thus facilitating a precise exchange of spiritual information.

We may ask, "If one should attain the spiritual root first, how can a beginner master this science without correct understanding of the teacher?" The answer is that through the great desire for spirituality, the student finds the right way and acquires the sensation of the Upper World. This is done by studying authentic sources only, as well as by detaching from any material rituals.

CHAPTER 2
THE PURPOSE OF KABBALAH

Kabbalists assert that the purpose of Creation is to bring joy and pleasure to the created beings. The will to enjoy (the vessel or the soul) receives pleasure according to the intensity of its desire.

This is why all that was created in all the worlds is merely a changing desire to receive pleasure, and the Creator satisfies this desire. This will to receive pleasure is the substance of Creation, both spiritual and corporeal, including that which already exists and that which will manifest in the future.

Matter in its diverse manifestations (minerals, plants, human beings, colors, sounds, etc.) is simply differing amounts of the will to receive pleasure. The Light emanated by the Creator vitalizes and fulfills such matter. Originally, both the desire to enjoy—called a "vessel"—and the desire to bring enjoyment—called the "Light"—corresponded with each other in magnitude. That is, the vessel (the will to enjoy) received maximum pleasure.

However, as the desire diminished, both the vessel and the Light that filled it gradually contracted and kept moving away from the Creator until they reached the lowest level, where the will to enjoy finally materialized.

The only difference between the Upper World and ours lies in the fact that in our world the vessel (the will to receive pleasure) exists at its lowest level, called the "material body."

Before its final materialization, the vessel evolves through four stages, divided into ten *Sefirot* (levels): *Keter, Hochma, Bina, Hesed, Gevura, Tifferet, Netzah, Hod, Yesod,* and *Malchut.* These *Sefirot* constitute filters inhibiting the Light that the Creator directs to the created beings. The task of these filters is to weaken the Light to such an extent that the creatures existing in our world will be able to perceive it.

Sefirat (singular for *Sefirot*) *Keter* is also called "the world *Adam Kadmon*"; *Sefirat Hochma* is called "the world *Atzilut*"; *Sefirat Bina*—"the world *Beria*"; the *Sefirot Hesed* to *Yesod*—"the world *Yetzira*"; and *Sefirat Malchut*—"the world *Assiya*." The last level of the world, *Assiya*, constitutes our universe (see Drawing 1).

Keter — Adam Kadmon
Hochma — Atzilut
Bina — Beria
Hesed ⎫
Gevura ⎪
Tifferet ⎬ — Yetzira
Netzah ⎪
Hod ⎪
Yesod ⎭
Upper Malchut — Assiya
....
Lower Malchut — Our Universe

Drawing 1

Kabbalah calls this level "*Olam ha Zeh*" (this world). It is perceived by those who exist in it, and the vessel, or the will to enjoy, is called "the body." The Light, called "pleasure," is perceived as the force of life.

Although the Light that fills the body is reduced so that we do not feel its source, by observing certain Creator-given rules described in Kabbalah, we purify ourselves from egoism and gradually ascend through all the worlds back to the Source.

As we attain higher spiritual levels, we receive larger portions of Light until we reach levels where we can receive all the Light (absolute, infinite delight) that was destined for us from the dawn of Creation.

Every soul is surrounded by spiritual Light. Although beginners in Kabbalah may not understand what they are studying in the authentic sources, their powerful desire to understand evokes the Upper Force that surrounds them, and the effects of this Upper Force purify and thus elevate them.

If not in this life, then in the next, every person will feel the need to study Kabbalah and to receive knowledge about the Creator.

The Light surrounds the human soul from the outside until one reaches a spiritual level where the Light begins to permeate it. The reception of the Light within depends only on one's desire and readiness, and on the purity of one's soul.

However, during one's studies one utters the names of the Sefirot, the worlds, and the spiritual actions connected to one's soul. Thus, the soul receives micro-doses of Light from the outside, a light that gradually purifies the soul and prepares it to receive spiritual energy and delight.

CHAPTER 3
THE GIVING OF KABBALAH

The great sage, Rabbi Akiva, (1st century CE) said: "Love thy neighbor as thyself is the comprehensive rule of all the spiritual laws."

As we know, the term "comprehensive" points to the sum of its constituents. Therefore, when Rabbi Akiva speaks about love for our neighbor (one of many spiritual laws), about our duties with regard to society and even to the Creator as the comprehensive law, he implies that all the other laws are mere constituents of this rule.

However, when we try to find an explanation for this, we are met with an even more unusual statement by the sage, Hillel. When his disciple asked him to teach him the entire wisdom of Kabbalah while standing on one foot, Hillel replied: "Anything that you hate, do not do to others!"

Hillel's answer teaches us that the whole purpose, indeed the reason for the existence of Kabbalah, is to clarify and fulfill a single law: "Love thy neighbor as thyself." Yet, how can I love another as myself? Loving others as myself would imply constantly fulfilling all the desires of all the people, when I am unable to satisfy even my own desires! Moreover, the sages explain that we have to satisfy others' desires *before* our own.

For example, it is written *(Tosfot, Masechet Kidushin)* that if you have only one pillow, you must give it to your friend, or if you have one chair, another person should take it, while you stand or sit on the ground. Otherwise, you will not be fulfilling the instruction of loving your neighbor. Is this a feasible demand? Since "Love thy neighbor as thyself" is the comprehensive law of Kabbalah, let's first find out what Kabbalah is.

Kabbalah teaches that the world and we, its dwellers, were created only to fulfill the laws that aim at humanity's spiritual development above our material world. In this way, we may attain similarity and unity with the Creator.

Yet, why did the Creator need to create us so corrupted and give us Kabbalah for our correction? *The Book of Zohar* answers this question in the following way: "He who eats someone else's bread is ashamed of looking in the giver's eyes."

Therefore, the world was created to save us from this shame. By struggling with our own egoism and correcting it, we will earn our future world.

To explain this, let's imagine the following situation: A rich man meets his poor friend, whom he has not seen for a long time. He brings him to his house, gives him food, drink, and clothes, day after day. One day, intending to please his friend, the rich man asks him what else he can do for him. The poor man's reply is: "I wish only one thing: to receive everything you are giving me out of mercy, as a reward for my own labor. You can fulfill all my desires except this one!"

We see how the giver is unable to rid the receiver of shame. On the contrary, the more favors the poor man receives, the greater his shame. The universe, our small planet, and human society (our workplace) were created to save us from this feeling. Our work is to return to the Creator with corrected desires and to receive a well-earned reward, the enormous delight of eternity, perfection, and merging with the Creator.

But why do we feel embarrassed and ashamed when receiving something from another? Scientists know the law of cause and effect. It states that every consequence is close in character to its cause, or source, and all the laws effective in the source are passed on to its consequence.

The effect of this law manifests at all levels of nature: inanimate, vegetative, animate, and human. The state of any mineral is determined by the laws that control it. We are accustomed to, and prefer, what we experience while growing up. Similarly, every particle that constitutes the consequence of a whole is drawn to its origin, and everything that is absent in the root is disliked and negated by its consequence.

Accordingly, since the Creator of nature is the Root and the Source of all that was created, we perceive all the laws effective within Him as pleasant, and all that is absent in Him as utterly alien and unattractive. For example, we like rest and dislike movement so much that we move only with the purpose of achieving rest. This is because the Root (Creator) from which we all originated is absolutely motionless. Hence, any motion is opposite to our nature.

We are born and we grow as absolute egoists, caring only for ourselves. Being egoists is what makes us opposite from the Creator, who vitalizes all nature. However, as we fall under the influence of society, we begin to understand the need for mutual aid, though its measure and direction depend on the society's level of development.

By creating our ill will (evil inclination) and by giving us Kabbalah as a counterbalance, the Creator enabled us to eliminate the manifestation of egoism and attain delight without shame.

There are two kinds of laws in Kabbalah—those with regard to other people and those with regard to the Creator. However, both of them are intended to make us similar to the Creator. It is utterly unimportant to us whether we act for the sake of the Creator or for the sake of other people. This is because anything that transcends the boundaries of our personal interest remains completely imperceptible.

Every movement that we make for the sake of another is—in the end—for self-benefit. It is absolutely impossible to make any physical or mental movement without a prior intention to derive at least some profit from it. This law of nature is known as "absolute egoism." Only by observing the spiritual laws can one achieve the state of selfless love for others. Those who do not follow the rules of Kabbalah have no way of transcending the boundaries of "absolute egoism."

According to Kabbalah, the laws regulating social relationships are more important than the laws regulating the relationship with the Creator. This is so because when we follow these laws under changing social circumstances, we are able to correct ourselves effectively and in the right direction.

Now we can understand Hillel's answer to his disciple: the main thing is to love your neighbor, the rest are merely subsidiary laws, including those pertaining to our relations with the Creator. In fact, one cannot merge with Him prior to attaining love for others. Hence, the ancient sage pointed to "love thy neighbor" as the safest and quickest means to master Kabbalah.

Now imagine a nation with a population of millions in which every member lovingly and unreservedly aspired to help every other member of society and satisfied their every need. Clearly, not a single person of that society would need to worry about him or herself or fear the future. Indeed, millions of loving people would constantly stand guard over their interests and take care of them.

However, since the nation would depend on its members, a breach in the obligation would create a vacuum in society because someone would remain without help. The bigger the number of violators, the more the rule that every member of society is obliged to observe would be breached. All are responsible for one another, both for observing the laws and for violating them.

Another ancient sage, Elazar, the son of Rashbi (Rabbi Shimon Bar-Yochai, the author of *The Zohar*), has an even greater surprise for us. He says that not only every nation, but all of humanity, every living being, is responsible for each other. Elazar states that all nations will have to observe this rule, and in so doing the entire world will be corrected. The world cannot be completely corrected and elevated unless everyone embraces the comprehensive law of the universe.

CHAPTER 4
PERFECTION AND THE WORLD

As we already know, the essence of the Creator's law lies in love, in maximum attention and compassion for all members of society, as for oneself. Let us see if we accept the Creator's law on faith alone or if some practical experimentation is needed here as well.

It is my hope that readers will understand my dislike for empty philosophy, because whole structures are built, and completely unsubstantiated conclusions are drawn, based on false conclusions. Our generation has seen many such philosophies put into practice. When basic theoretical assumptions prove to be faulty, the entire theory collapses and can immerse millions in torment.

Can we wish to fulfill the Creator's law by studying the world and its laws on the basis of practically obtained data? When we observe the order that exists in nature, we are struck by the precision of its governance at both micro and macro levels. For example, let us take the creatures closest to us—human beings. A cell that comes from a father and arrives at a prepared, reliable place in a mother, receives everything necessary for its development until it emerges into this world. Nothing can harm it until it starts its existence as a separate organism.

When it does emerge, nature carefully arouses the necessary feelings in the parents to give the child absolute confidence in their love and care. Humans, as well as animals and plants, multiply and then take care of their offspring's development.

However, a dramatic contradiction exists between the way nature takes care of the birth and the early, independent development of a species and its later struggle for survival. This striking contradiction in how the world is governed, which exists at all levels of life, has captivated human minds since ancient times and has generated several theories:

Evolution: This theory does not consider it necessary to explain the above-mentioned contradiction. The Creator created the world and rules over everything. He is insensitive, unable to think, and creates the species in accordance with physical laws. The created species develops in conformity with evolution, meaning the harsh laws of survival. This theory refers to the Creator as "nature," thereby emphasizing its insensitivity.

Dualism: Since nature's striking wisdom exceeds by far humankind's ability, it is impossible to predict and design future organisms without feedback. The giver (nature) should also possess intellect, memory, and feelings. Indeed, one cannot assert that every level of nature is ruled by mere chance.

This theory has led to the conclusion that two forces exist, positive and negative, and that both forces possess intellect and feelings. Hence, these forces are capable of endowing everything they create with those faculties. The development of this theory led to the creation of several other theories.

Polytheism: The analysis of nature's actions and the division of its forces according to their character brought forth religions (such as that of ancient Greek) that included an assembly of deities, each governed by a certain force.

Absence of governance: With the appearance of precise instruments and new methods, research has lately discovered a close connection between all parts of the world. Therefore, the theory about a multitude of forces was discarded and was replaced with an assumption about a wise, unified force that guides the world. However, due to humanity's insignificance, compared to the greatness of this force, we are left unattended.

Alas, humanity continues to suffer regardless of the numerous theories about the world's creation and governance. It is incomprehensible why nature is so gentle in the mother's womb and during early childhood, and so ruthless in adulthood, when we seemingly need its help even more. A question arises: Are we not the reason for nature's cruelty toward the world?

All of nature's actions are interconnected; hence, by violating one of its laws, we upset the balance of the entire system. It does not matter whether we speak of nature as a heartless, purposeless guide or as a Creator with a plan, a goal, and wisdom. We exist in a world of certain laws, and by violating them we are punished with the corrupted environment, society, and our corrupted selves. Besides, since nature's laws are interconnected, breaking one of them may cause us to suffer an unexpected, harsh blow from a different direction.

Nature, or the Creator (which are actually the same), influences us through certain laws, which we are obliged to regard as objective and compulsory, and thus follow them. We must understand nature's laws, because failing to follow them is the cause of all our sufferings.

It is common knowledge that humans are social beings. We cannot survive without the assistance of others in the society. Thus, one who suddenly decides to isolate oneself from society will be subject to a life of suffering because that person will be unable to provide for his or her needs.

Nature obliges us to live among others like us, and by communicating with them, carry out two operations: to receive everything needed from society, and to give the society the product of our labors. Violating either rule upsets the balance in society and therefore deserves society's punishment.

In the case of excessive reception (such as stealing), society's penalty quickly follows. Should a person refuse to serve society, punishment, as a rule, does not follow at all or is not directly related to the transgression. This is why the condition that obliges one to provide a service to society is usually ignored. Nature, however, acts as an unbiased judge and punishes humanity according to its development.

Kabbalah maintains that the sequence of generations in the world is merely the appearance and disappearance of protein-based bodies, whereas the soul that fulfills the "I" changes its carrier without disappearing. The circulation of the constant and limited number of souls, their descent to our world and appearance in new bodies, provides us with new generations of people. Therefore, with regard to the souls, all generations, from the first to the last, are considered one generation. It is of no importance whatsoever how many times each soul goes in and out of various bodies. For the sake of comparison, the death of the body has absolutely no effect on the soul, just as cut hair or clipped nails have no effect on the life of a body.

By creating the worlds and giving them to us, the Creator has placed a goal before us: to reach His level and to bond with Him by climbing up the worlds He has built. The question is, must humanity feel obliged to fulfill His will?

Kabbalah reveals a complete, closed picture of the Creator's control over us. Thus, willingly or spurred by suffering, in this lifetime or in a subsequent life, influenced by physical, social, and economic factors, every one of us and all of humanity will have to accept the purpose of Creation as our life's objective.

In the end, all will attain a single goal. The only difference lies in the path: a person who willingly and consciously advances towards the goal gains twofold: saving time and experiencing the delight of merging with the Creator, instead of suffering.

The gravity of the situation is that humanity does not yet imagine the calamities that lie ahead of it. The goal has been set and the laws of the universe are invariable. Personal everyday sufferings and periodic global catastrophes are making every one of us acknowledge the need to observe the Creator's law—to annul egoism and envy and instead develop compassion, mutual aid, and love.

CHAPTER 5
FREEDOM OF WILL

The concept of freedom determines our whole life. Animals in captivity usually develop ill health and may even die—a sure sign that nature disagrees with any kind of subjugation. It is not by chance that for centuries humanity engaged in bloodshed and battles to obtain a certain measure of freedom.

Even so, we have a rather vague idea about freedom and independence. We assume that everyone has an inner need for freedom and independence, and that they are available to us at will. But if we examine our actions carefully, we will discover that we act compulsively and that we have no free will at all.

Such a statement requires explaining: Externally, a human being is guided by two reins: pleasure or pain (also defined as "happiness" or "suffering").

Animals have no free choice. Humankind's advantage over animals is that people consciously prefer to endure pain if they believe that pleasure awaits at its end. Thus, a sick person agrees to a painful operation, trusting that this will improve his or her health.

However, this choice is merely a pragmatic calculation in which one compares future pleasure to present pain. In other words, this calculation is a simple mathematical operation in which the amount of suffering is subtracted from the future pleasure, and the difference dictates the choice. If the achieved pleasure is less than the anticipated pleasure, a person suffers, instead of feeling joy.

The force of attraction to delight and retraction from pain is the only force that controls humans, animals, and even the vegetative. All living creatures at all stages and levels of life are governed by it; hence, in that sense there is no difference between them, since free will does not depend on intelligence.

Furthermore, even the selection of the *type* of pleasure is mandatory and does not depend of one's free choice. Instead, our choices are dictated by society's norms and tastes, not by one's free choice. It follows that there is no such thing as an independent individual who has personal freedom of action.

People who believe in Upper Governance expect reward or punishment for their actions in the next world. Atheists expect it in this world. Because they expect reward or punishment for their actions, they think that they have freedom of choice.

The root of this phenomenon lies in the law of cause and effect that influences nature as a whole and every individual in particular. In other words, all four kinds of Creation—inanimate, vegetative, animate, and human—are continually influenced by the law of causality and purpose. Their every state is determined by the influence of external causes with regard to the predetermined goal chosen by them, which is the future state.

Every object in the world is constantly developing. This implies that every object constantly abandons previous forms and acquires new ones under the influence of four factors:

1. Origin
2. Evolution that stems from its own nature and is therefore invariable
3. Evolution that changes under the influence of external factors
4. Evolution and transformation of external factors

The first factor is the origin or the primary matter, its previous form. Since every object constantly changes form, each previous form is defined as "primary" with regard to the subsequent form. The inner properties depend solely on the origin, determine the subsequent form, and constitute its main factor, its individual information, gene or property.

The second factor is the order of cause-and-effect development that depends on the origin of the object. This order does not change. An example is a grain of wheat that decays in the soil and, as a result, produces a new shoot. The wheat grain loses its original form, meaning it completely disappears and acquires a new form of a shoot that will produce a new initial form, a wheat grain, as such is its origin. Only the number of grains, and possibly their quality (size and taste) may change. In other words, one can observe the cause-and-effect order where everything depends on the origin of the object.

The third factor is the cause-and-effect connection in the primary matter, which changes its properties after contact with external forces. Consequently, the quantity and quality of the grain change because additional factors (soil, water, sun) appear to complement the properties of the primary matter.

Since the force of the origin prevails over the additional factors, the changes may modify the grain's quality, but not the species itself, such as turning a wheat grain into a barley grain. In other words, like the second factor, the third factor is the object's inner factor, but unlike the second, it can change qualitatively and quantitatively.

The fourth factor is the cause-and-effect connection between the forces that act on the outside, such as chance, the elements of nature, and neighbors. For the most part, these four factors together influence every individual object.

The first factor (origin) is fundamental for us because we are creations of our parents. As their offspring, we (in a sense) are their copies; i.e., almost all the attributes of the parents and grandparents manifest themselves in their children. The concepts and knowledge acquired by the ancestors manifest in the descendants as habits and properties, even at an unconscious level. The concealed forces of heredity drive all of the descendants' actions and are passed from generation to generation.

This gives rise to various inclinations that can be observed in people: faith, criticism, material comforts, stinginess, or modesty. None of them is an acquired property; rather, they are a heritage of close and distant ancestors registered in the offspring's brain.

Since we automatically inherit the acquired properties of our ancestors, these properties resemble a grain that loses its form in the soil. Yet, some of our acquired properties manifest within us in an opposite way.

Because primary matter manifests in forces without external form, this matter may carry both positive and negative properties.

The three other factors influence us as well. The order of causes and their consequences that ensue from one's origin (the 2nd factor) is invariable. A grain decays under the influence of the environment and gradually changes its form until a new grain manifests. In other words, the first factor acquires the form of primary matter; the difference between the previous plant and the new shoot manifests only in quantity and quality.

By coming to this world, a person falls under the influence of society against his or her will and takes in society's character and properties. Thus, one's hereditary inclinations are transformed under the influence of society.

The third factor is based on the influence of the environment. Every one of us knows how our tastes and views can sometimes be reversed under the influence of society. Nothing like that can occur at the inanimate, vegetative, or animate levels of nature; this can happen only with humans.

The fourth factor is the direct and indirect influence of negative external factors (troubles and anxiety) that have nothing to do with the consecutive order of development of the primary matter.

All our thoughts and actions depend on these four factors and dictate our entire way of life. Just like clay in the hands of the potter, we are under the influence of these four factors. We therefore see that there is no freedom of desire, that everything depends solely on the interaction between these four factors, and that we can have no control. No scientific theory answers how the spiritual governs matter from within, and where or what mediates between the body and the soul.

Kabbalah says that all that was ever created in all the worlds consists only of the Light and the vessel it fills. The only creation is the vessel that wishes to receive the Light coming directly from the Creator. This will to receive the Light that brings life and pleasure to the vessel is both the spiritual and the corporeal substance, depending on one's intensity of desire.

The differences in nature, quality, and quantity among all created beings lie only in the extent of this desire, which is accordingly filled with the Light coming from the life-giving Creator.

All that separates one object from another and produces colors, substances, waves, and other differentiating factors results from the capacity of the will to receive, and therefore, of the amount of Light that fills it. In other words, a desire of one size yields the form of a mineral; different sizes of desires form liquids, colors, or waves. Everything depends on the position on the scale of desire, while the amount of Light that embraces us and all the worlds is equal and invariable.

Now we can clarify the question about freedom of the individual. Since we already understand that an individual consists of a will to receive a certain quantity of the Creator's Light, all the traits peculiar to that desire depend solely on the intensity of this desire, on the force of the attraction of the Light.

The attraction force we usually call "ego" compels us to struggle for our existence. If we destroy one of the ego's desires or aspirations, we deny it the opportunity to use its potential "vessel," the fulfillment of which is its Creator-given right.

We acquire all our ideas through the influence of our environment, for a grain develops only in its soil, in the environment that suits it. Hence, the only choice we have in life is the choice of our society, our circle of friends. By changing our environment, we necessarily change our views because an individual is merely a copy, a product of his or her society.

People who realize this conclude that one has no freedom of will because one is a product of society and one's thought does not manage one's body. Rather, the external information is stored in the brain's memory; and like a mirror, the brain merely reflects everything that occurs in the environment.

Our origin is our basic, primary material. We inherit our aspirations and inclinations, and this inheritance is the only thing that distinguishes one person from another. Everyone is influenced differently by society; this is why we will never find two identical people.

Know that this primary material is the individual's true wealth, and one should not try to modify it because, by developing one's unique traits, a person becomes a personality.

Therefore, a person who does away with even a single impulse or aspiration creates emptiness in the world; this impulse or aspiration will never be repeated in any other body. From this we see what a crime "civilized nations" commit by forcing their culture on other nations and by destroying their foundations.

Yet, is it possible to ensure complete individual freedom in a society? Clearly, to function normally, society must impose its laws, restrictions, and norms on individuals. It follows that one is in a constant struggle with one's society. Here arises an even sharper point: if the majority has the right to dictate society's rules, and the masses are always less developed than the most developed persons in society, this would create regression instead of progress.

If a society establishes its laws in accordance with spiritual laws, those who observe them do not lose an opportunity as an individual to merge with the Creator. This is because these laws are the natural laws of governance over the world and society. If a society creates its own laws, which contradict the laws of the spiritual nature, those who observe spiritual laws will achieve their maximum development.

According to the purposeful governance, we must observe the laws of nature so that individuals and society will develop in the right direction. Kabbalah instructs that we make all decisions according to society's opinion. Kabbalah shows us that in daily life we must accept the opinion of the majority, and in spiritual development we must follow the opinion of developed individuals.

This rule is called the "natural law of governance." All the rules and laws of the science of Kabbalah comprise the laws of nature's governance. While studying the interconnections between the laws that influence our world from Above downward through Kabbalah, it becomes clear that the law of the majority's influence in the society is a natural one.

CHAPTER 6
THE ESSENCE AND THE PURPOSE OF KABBALAH

- What is the essence of Kabbalah?
- Is the purpose of Kabbalah aimed at life in this world or in the future one?
- Who benefits from Kabbalah, the Creator or His creatures?

Kabbalists who attain the Creator feel that He is absolutely kind. They explain that He cannot cause even the slightest pain to anyone in the world because egoism, the will to enjoy for oneself, the cause of every unpleasant sensation, is absent in Him.

We do harm to others for the sole purpose of satisfying our own want for something. If this feeling did not have a constant grip on man, there would be no foundation for evil in the world. Since we perceive the Creator as absolutely perfect and whole, the absence of the will to "acquire" in Him leads to the absence of any evil in Him.

If this is the case, then He should appear to us as absolutely kind, a sensation that seizes every one of us in moments of joy, delight, and fulfillment. However, since everything we feel comes from the Creator, all of His creatures should feel only good and kindness... And what do we feel instead?!

The whole of nature consists of four levels: inanimate, vegetative, animate, and human. Each level undergoes purposeful development: slow, gradual, cause-and-effect growth. This resembles a fruit growing on a tree that becomes appealing and edible only at the end of its ripening.

Yet, how many intermediate states has the fruit gone through from the beginning to the end of its growth? The intermediate states reveal nothing about the fruit's final condition, when it becomes mellow and sweet. Rather, the opposite occurs: as good as the ripe fruit is at its end, so is it bitter and hard during its ripening.

The same occurs in the animal world: an animal's mental capacity is limited in maturity, but while it grows, its limitations are inconspicuous compared to those of a human child. For example, a one-day-old calf has all the properties of a fully grown bull. Then, it practically stops developing, which makes it opposite to human beings, who acquire intelligence in the prime of life, but are utterly helpless and pitiful in the first years of life.

The difference is so striking that by looking at a newborn calf and a newborn baby, one who is unfamiliar with the ways of our world would conclude that nothing worthwhile will come from a human baby, whereas a calf will, at the very least, grow up to be a new Napoleon.

As a rule, intermediate states are opposite to the final outcome. Therefore, only one who knows the final outcome will accept and understand the unappealing form of the object during its development. This is why people often draw the wrong conclusions, failing to foresee the final outcome.

In fact, the Creator's ways of governing our world are purposeful and manifest only at the end of development. In His attitude toward us, the Creator is guided by the principle of "absolute good," without a trace of evil; and the purpose of His governance is evidenced in our gradual development. Finally, we will become able to receive all the goodness that was prepared for us. Surely, this goal will be achieved in accordance with His plan.

Two paths of development in the right direction are prepared for us:

- A path of suffering that compels us to escape it. We do not see the goal and are forced to run away from the pain. This path is called "unconscious evolution," or "a path of pain."

- The path of conscious, painless, and quick spiritual development by following the Kabbalistic method, which facilitates a quick attainment of the desirable result.

The purpose of all the laws of development using the method of Kabbalah is to recognize the good and evil within us, and develop recognition of evil. By observing the spiritual laws, we can rid ourselves of all evil. This is because the difference in one's development creates either a deeper, or a more superficial, recognition of evil, and a more powerful or less powerful desire to be rid of it.

The source of all evil is our egoism because it is opposite to the nature of the Creator, who wishes to bestow only good upon us. Since all that we perceive as pleasant comes personally from Him, proximity to the Creator is perceived as pleasure, and the degree of remoteness from Him is proportionally perceived as suffering.

Because the Creator hates egoism, humans, too, abhor it, depending on the extent of their development. Attitudes towards egoism are wide-ranging, from acceptance of egoism as normal in a spiritually undeveloped person who uses it without restriction (down to stealing and murdering openly), to a more developed person's feeling of shame because of open displays of egoism, to actual revulsion towards egoism in a spiritually developed individual.

Thus, we find that the answers to the original questions are as follows:

- The essence of Kabbalah lies in enabling a person to attain the ultimate level of development without suffering, and in a positive way.

- The purpose of Kabbalah is to attain the ultimate level, depending on the spiritual work that a person has done on him or herself in this world.

- Kabbalah was not given to the created beings for their well being; it was given as an instruction for self-perfection.

CHAPTER 7
FROM THE AFTERWORD TO THE ZOHAR

Kabbalah explains that the correct, consistent observance of spiritual laws leads to adhesion with the Creator. Yet, what does the word "adhesion" mean? Indeed, because of the limits of time, a three-dimensional space, and bodily desires, our thoughts cannot grasp the Creator. Therefore, as long our thoughts are bound by these limits, we cannot be objective.

As we transcend our egos, the will to receive and the definitions of time, space, and motion change. They acquire a spiritual dimension. In that state, we control our will to receive and are not governed by it. Therefore, our thoughts do not depend on the will to receive, and hence are objective.

As a result, Kabbalah offers the attainment of equivalence of properties and actions with the Creator as a means of nearing Him. It says: merge with His actions; be as kind, caring, and as humble as He. Yet, how can one be sure that the Creator's actions and the Creator Himself are the same? Moreover, why should I merge with Him by imitating His actions?

In the material world, we imagine merging, or adhesion, as shortening the distance between bodies, and understand separation as moving away from one another. However, the spiritual realm lacks such concepts as time, space, and motion. This is why the equivalence of properties between two spiritual objects draws them closer to one another, and the difference in properties moves them apart. There can be no adhesion or separation (in contrast to the adhesion or separation in space) because the spiritual object itself takes no place.

Just as an axe divides a physical object, the appearance of a new property in a spiritual object divides it into two parts. That is, if the difference in properties is insignificant, then the spiritual objects are close to one another. The bigger the distinction between their properties, the more remote they are from one another. If they love each other, they are spiritually "close," and the distance between their corporeal shells is unimportant. The relationship between them is determined by their spiritual affinity.

If one likes something that is disliked by another, the distance between them depends on the difference in their views and sensations. They are considered completely opposite if one of them likes everything the other hates.

Thus, we see that in the spiritual world (the world of desires), similarity or difference in aspirations, desires, ideas, and properties plays the role of an axe, dividing the spiritual into parts. The distance between spiritual objects is determined by the extent of incongruence between their sensations and properties.

Therefore, by following the Creator's will, feelings, and thoughts, we approach Him. Since the Creator acts only for the sake of His created beings, we, too, have to wish our fellow beings well and be good to all of them. Since we exist in the material world, the necessary minimum for the existence of the body is not considered a manifestation of egoism.

Can we do good to others with absolute selflessness? After all, the Creator created us as absolute egoists, possessing a will to enjoy. We cannot transform our nature, and even by being good to each other, we will consciously or subconsciously try to derive benefit for ourselves. Unless we see any self-profit, we are unable to make even the slightest movement for the sake of another.

Indeed, people are powerless to change their nature of absolute egoism, let alone transform it into something completely opposite (being good without receiving honor, rest, fame, health, or money in return). This is why the method of observing the spiritual laws through Kabbalah was given. There is no other means by which our nature can be changed.

The body and its organs make a single whole and constantly exchange sensations and information. For example, if the body feels that one of its parts can improve the general condition of the whole body, that particular part immediately feels it and fulfills this will. In case some body part suffers, the whole body instantly knows about it and tries to improve the situation.

From this example, one can understand man's state, or rather, the state of the soul that attains unity with the Creator. Before dressing in the body, the soul is seemingly a single whole with the Creator. However, once dressed in the body, it completely separates itself from Him due to the difference between the properties of the Creator and those of the body.

This means that by imparting the sensation of egoism to the soul, the Creator created something else besides Himself, because different desires separate objects in the spiritual world. Therefore, the object (the soul) and the egoism (the body) become separate parts. Similarly, man is remote from the Creator, like an organ that was cut off from the body. They are so distant from each other that man does not feel the Creator at all. Indeed, the distance is so great that he can only *believe* in Him, not *know* Him.

Hence, if we attain unity with the Creator by making our properties equivalent to His (i.e., by observing the spiritual laws and transforming egoism, which separates us from the Creator, into altruism), we attain His thoughts and desires. We also reveal the secrets of Kabbalah, as the Creator's thoughts are the secrets of the universe!

There are two parts to Kabbalah: revealed and hidden. Both constitute the Creator's thoughts. Kabbalah is like a rope thrown from above to a drowning person in a sea of egoism. By observing spiritual laws, a person prepares for the second, main stage when the one who observes and the one who obliges spiritually merge.

Those who observe spiritual rules go through five levels: *Nefesh*, *Ruach*, *Neshama*, *Haya*, and *Yechida*. Each level consists of five sub-levels, which are then divided into five additional sub-levels. In all, the ladder of spiritual ascent, or closeness to the Creator, consists of 125 steps. The five main steps of this ladder are called "worlds." Their sub-levels are called *Partzufim*, which consist of *Sefirot*.

All that exists in a certain spiritual world perceives the objects in that world and below it. However, they cannot even imagine or feel anything from a higher world. Therefore, one who reaches one of the 125 levels attains all the souls that exist there from the past, present, and future generations and remains there with them. We, who exist only in our world, are unable to imagine or feel anything existing at other levels or other worlds, including those that populate them.

Kabbalists that reach a certain level on their path to the Creator can describe that level with expressions that only people who attained it can understand. Those who have not attained the described level can be confused by such descriptions and be led away from the correct understanding.

As was said above, our path to the Creator is divided into 125 levels/degrees, but one cannot ascend all of them prior to completing one's correction. There are two distinctions between all the generations and the last, completely corrected one:

1. Only in the last generation will it be possible to attain all 125 levels.

2. In past generations, only a few people could attain the other worlds. In the last generation, everyone will be able to ascend through the spiritual levels and merge with the Creator.

The term "last generation" refers to all human generations from 1995 onward because, according to *The Book of Zohar,* that was the time when humankind entered a new phase—that of The Final Correction. In Kabbalah, this period is also called the "time of deliverance," when humanity is destined to come out of the lowest state.

Rashbi and his disciples ascended all 125 levels. This is why they were able to write *The Book of Zohar*, which encompasses all 125 levels of the worlds. It is therefore said in *The Zohar* that the book will be revealed only at "the end of days," meaning on the eve of the end of correction. Other generations couldn't reach the end of correction. Thus, they could not understand this book because they were unable to surmount all 125 levels from which the *Book of Zohar* is written. In our generation, we can all reach the 125th level; at that time, we can all understand the *Book of Zohar*.

The fact that a contemporary Kabbalist succeeded in fully commenting on the *Book of Zohar* is a sign that we are on the threshold of the last generation, and that anyone can understand the *Book of Zohar*. Indeed, not a single commentary on the *Book of Zohar* appeared before our time. Today, we have available to us the clear, complete *Sulam* commentary on the *Book of Zohar* written by Baal HaSulam, just as it should be in the last generation.

However, we should understand that spiritual actions do not occur the way physical actions do: that is, cause and effect do not directly follow. In our time, the spiritual state of the worlds is ready for the coming of the Messiah (the force that pulls Creation out of egoism and leads it to altruism). Yet, this merely gives us an opportunity for attainment, whereas actual attainment depends on us and our spiritual levels.

We can unite with the Creator by equalizing our properties, desires, and goals with His, by completely destroying egoism and selflessly doing good things. However, a question arises: where will a complete egoist (one unable to make a spiritual or physical movement unless it offers personal benefits) find the strength and motivation to live for the sake of others?

The answer to this question can be easily understood with an example from life:

Imagine a situation in which you wholeheartedly wish to give a present to someone who is important in your eyes, someone you love and respect. Suppose this person agrees to accept your gift, or agrees to come to your home for dinner.

Although you spend money and work hard to treat the important guest well, you enjoy it as if it is not you, but the guest who does you a favor, giving and entertaining you by consenting to accept your treat. Hence, if we could imagine the Creator as someone we respect, we would gladly please Him.

We can observe the laws of the universe only if we attain the Creator's greatness. Then, when we work for His sake and realize His grandeur, it is as though we receive from Him. Yet, since thoughts depend on the influence of society and social environments, everything that society praises also becomes elevated in the eyes of the individual. Hence, the most important thing is to be among as many people who exalt the Creator as possible.

If our environment does not elevate the Creator to the proper level, it will not allow us to attain spirituality. A student should feel like the smallest of all the students. In this way, the student can absorb society's views, and in that state, the student considers society's views as important. For this reason comes the truism, "Buy for yourself a friend." Indeed, the more people influence me with their opinions, the more diligently I will be able to work on myself, on correcting my egoism, in order to feel the Creator.

It is said that every person should attain the Root, the source of his or her soul. In other words, the final goal should be to completely merge with the Creator. The Creator's properties are referred to as *Sefirot*. This is why, while studying the *Sefirot* and their actions, it is as though we learn these properties, merge with them, unite with the Creator's mind, and become one with the Creator.

The importance of Kabbalah stems from the fact that by studying it, we learn how the worlds were created and how they are governed. By studying the Creator's actions and properties, we discover what we should be like in order to unite with Him.

CHAPTER 8
THE LANGUAGE OF KABBALAH

Because our vocabulary is limited by our perception of the world, which is connected to the concepts of time, space, and motion, we have no words to express or convey spiritual concepts. We have developed our whole vocabulary from being in this world, and thus, if we want to use mundane words to name spiritual phenomena, such words are inadequate.

It is difficult to find words that explain the experience of spirituality to someone who has never felt it. Although we may want to describe a spiritual object, we have only corporeal words to name it. If even a single concept does not find precise correspondence in words, the correct meaning of the entire science will be ruined. Thus, the problem of relating to the spiritual world without the appropriate words or language to describe it remains unsolved.

Every object and action in our world originates from a corresponding one in the spiritual world. Therefore, Kabbalists have found a reliable way to convey information and knowledge to one another. They use the names of objects and actions (branches) in our material world to describe the corresponding objects and actions (roots) in the spiritual world.

This language was developed by people who attained the spiritual worlds while still living in our world, and accurately knew these correspondences. Hence, Kabbalists aptly named it "the language of the branches."

From this we can understand the odd names that we find in Kabbalistic books, the descriptions of actions that we perceive as odd stories or children's fairytales. Nevertheless, this language is very accurate because there is a precise and unique correspondence between each root and its branch.

It is no wonder that there is such a correspondence, as the creators of the language of the branches simultaneously existed in both the spiritual and the physical worlds. This is why it is impossible to replace even a single word, and however absurd it may seem, the branch should exactly correspond to the root.

What separates spiritual objects is not space, but their spiritual incongruence and dissimilarity of properties. Therefore, the number of souls, meaning separate spiritual objects, determines the number of people in the physical world.

In the beginning of Creation there was one common soul: the Light (pleasure) and the corresponding body (desire), *Adam*. These were merged in adhesion with the Creator, and therefore received maximum delight. The soul's nature is merely the will to receive pleasure, and the soul was filled with pleasure in accordance with its desire. However, once having received pleasure, the soul sensed shame. In our world, everyone who receives a gift or favor feels the same way.

The extent of the sense of shame depends on the person's spiritual development. Only this feeling keeps us constantly within limits and compels us to observe the laws of the society. The same sensation underlies our aspirations for knowledge, wealth, recognition by society, and honor.

Once it had felt a burning shame, corresponding to the received pleasure, the soul discovered that the only way to be rid of it was to stop enjoying the pleasure. However, since the Creator's desire was to delight the soul, the soul agreed to accept this delight--not for its own sake, but only for the sake of the Creator.

Just as in our world, the more pleasure the child receives from food, such as "eating for Mommy," the more delight it gives its parent. In this situation, the soul should constantly control the amount of pleasure it receives in order to enjoy only for the Creator's sake.

However, since the common soul could not instantly overcome its natural desire to enjoy for its own sake (that is how great it was!), it was shattered into myriad fragments (souls). These fragments were easier to work on, to neutralize the selfish will to enjoy.

Since no distance exists in the spiritual world, and proximity is determined by the similarity of actions and thoughts (affinity, love), souls that receive "for the Creator's sake" are close to Him because they please each other, just like a mother and her child.

Closeness is determined by how much pleasure the soul receives for the sake of the Creator. The will to receive instinctively acts within us, but our desire to rid ourselves of shame and to enjoy for the Creator's sake originates within us. Therefore, the desire to rid self of shame and to enjoy for the Creator's sake requires special and continuous effort.

The soul that receives for its own sake is opposite from the Giver in its intention and spiritual action. The greater the pleasure it selfishly receives, the greater its opposition to the Creator.

Since the difference in desires leads one away from the Creator, different worlds were formed at different levels of remoteness down to our world. Here, every part of the common soul is given a certain period of time (life span) and repeated opportunities (life cycles) for correction.

A person is born only with the will to receive pleasure for self. All our "personal" desires originate from the system of impure forces. In other words, we are infinitely remote from the Creator, we cannot feel Him, and are therefore considered "spiritually dead."

However, if, while struggling with oneself, a person acquires the desire to live, think, and act only for the sake of others and the Creator, such soul purification allows one to gradually approach the Creator until completely merging with Him. And as one comes closer to the Creator, one feels increasing delight.

It is for this soul transformation that our world and all the spiritual worlds (the steps on the path to the Creator) were created. Merging with the Creator is a task that everyone must accomplish while still living in our world.

Our world is the most opposite point from the Creator—opposite from His properties. By ridding ourselves of the selfish desire to enjoy, we approach Him and thus gain doubly: we enjoy receiving pleasure from Him and at the same time, enjoy pleasing Him. In the same way, when I eat my mother's food, I enjoy the meal and am glad it pleases her.

It should be noted that while egoistic pleasure is short-lived and limited by the size of the desire (we cannot eat two dinners), one can endlessly give, share, or receive for the sake of another. Accordingly, the pleasure that one receives is infinite!

Every world with all that populates it (including our world) unites in the Creator's single plan to bestow infinite delight upon the soul. This single thought, this goal, encompasses the entire Creation from beginning to end. All the suffering we feel, our work on ourselves, and the reward are determined only by this thought.

After the individual correction, all souls reunite into one soul as before. Thus, the pleasure received by each soul not only doubles from the reception of delight and pleasing the Creator, but it is multiplied by the number of reunited souls.

Meanwhile, as people who work on themselves ascend spiritually, their eyes begin to open and other worlds become visible. Thus, while still living in this world, they attain all the worlds. For them, the seemingly absurd language of Kabbalah becomes the language of actions, thoughts, and sensations; the concepts that are opposite in our world then unite in the single Supernal Root.

CHAPTER 9
FROM THE PREFACE TO THE ZOHAR

The *Book of Zohar* was concealed from the uninitiated from the day of its creation. Now, the conditions have ripened for its disclosure to the public. To make *The Zohar* accessible to every reader, we must precede it with some explanations.

First, it should be noted that everything described in *The Zohar* is an order of ten *Sefirot*: *Keter, Hochma, Bina, Hesed, Gevura, Tifferet, Netzah, Hod, Yesod, Malchut*, and their combinations. In the same way express any thought with a limited number of letters in the alphabet, so are the combinations of the ten *Sefirot* sufficient to describe every spiritual action or object.

However, there are three clear boundaries one should always keep in mind, connected to the four levels of perception (or attainment) in our world: Matter, Form in Matter, Abstract Form, and Essence. These four levels of attainment also exist in the ten *Sefirot*.

The first boundary: *The Zohar* researches only Matter and Form in Matter, but it in no way concerns itself with Abstract Form and Essence.

The second boundary: All that was created consists of three levels:

1. The world *Ein Sof* (Infinity);

2. The world *Atzilut*;

3. The worlds *Beria, Yetzira*, and *Assiya* (BYA).

The Zohar studies only the three last worlds *BYA*. It does not study the worlds *Ein Sof* and *Atzilut* in and of themselves, but only what the worlds *BYA* receive from *Atzilut* and *Ein Sof*.

The third boundary: Each of the worlds *BYA* consists of three levels:

- The Ten *Sefirot* that constitute the Creator's part in each world;
- Human souls;
- Everything else that exists: *Mala'achim* (angels), *Levushim* (dresses), and *Heichalot* (palaces).

The Book of Zohar studies human souls, whereas all other objects are analyzed only with respect to human souls. It is worth noting that all mistakes, inaccuracies, and delusions are the results of transcending these three boundaries.

The following *Sefirot* correspond to the four reviewed worlds—*Atzilut, Beria, Yetzira, Assiya* (ABYA):

- *Sefirat (Sefira of) Hochma* corresponds to the world *Atzilut*;
- *Sefirat Bina* corresponds to the world *Beria*;
- The six *Sefirot*, from *Hesed* to *Yesod*, collectively called *Tifferet*, correspond to the world *Yetzira*;
- *Sefirat Malchut* corresponds to the world *Assiya*.

All that exists above the world *Atzilut* refers to *Sefirat Keter*.

However, each of the above worlds is also divided into ten *Sefirot*. Even the most infinitesimal object in any of the worlds is divided into (or consists of) ten *Sefirot*.

The Zohar ascribes a specific color to each *Sefira* (Drawing 2 on next page):

- White corresponds to *Sefirat Hochma*;
- Red corresponds to *Sefirat Bina*;
- Green corresponds to *Sefirat Tifferet*; and
- Black corresponds to *Sefirat Malchut*.

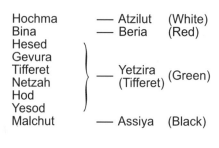

Drawing 2

Although the Light that fills the *Sefirot* is colorless, receivers see it with its corresponding hue. Thus, in all five worlds (from *Ein Sof* to our world), the Light that emanates from the Creator is an absolutely colorless, imperceptible substance. Only after it traverses the worlds and *Sefirot* as if through color filters do we perceive it as having a certain color and intensity, depending on the level of the soul that receives the Light.

For example, the world *Atzilut* passes the Light without coloring it at all because this world has similar properties to those of the Light. This is why the color of the Light in the world *Atzilut* is defined as white. The properties of other worlds differ from the properties of the Light; hence, each of them affects it depending on its spiritual closeness to the Light.

If we compare the white Light to paper, then the message written on it presents the information, and its color stands out against the white background. In the same way, by perceiving red, green, and black, we are able to perceive Light.

The world *Atzilut* (*Sefirat Hochma*) is the white background of the book, thus we are unable to conceive it. However, *Bina* (the world *Beria*), *Tifferet* (*Yetzira*), and *Malchut* (*Assiya*) that respectively correspond to red, green, and black, provide us with information based on their combinations, interactions, and reactions to the Light passing from the world *Atzilut* to our world.

Thus, it is as if the worlds *Beria*, *Yetzira*, and *Assiya* form concentric coverings of the world *Atzilut*. Now let us look into four kinds of the object's attainment—Matter, Form in Matter, Abstract Form, and Essence.

Suppose the object is a deceitful person:

- Matter is that person's body;

- Form in Matter is the property of deceitfulness;

- The Abstract Form is deceitfulness, as perceived regardless of the Matter;

- The person's Essence (which is absolutely inconceivable when separated from the body).

We cannot imagine the Essence *per se* with our sense organs, even when supplemented by any fantasy. We can attain only the actions and reactions to the surrounding reality, and the various interactions with the Essence. For instance, when we examine an object, the eye perceives not the object itself, but its interaction with the light, or rather the light's interaction with the eye. Our auditory sense perceives not the sound, but the interaction of the wave with our auditory sense. Our gustatory sense perceives not the object itself, but the interaction of saliva, nerve tips, and glands with an object.

All our sensations reveal only the interactions of the Essence's reactions, not the Essence itself. Even our tactile sense, which provides us with information of an object's hardness and temperature, does not reveal the object itself, but enables us to judge it based solely on our reaction to touching and sensing it.

Thus, the maximum attainment of the world lies in researching how the Essence influences us. However, since even in our wildest fantasies we cannot imagine the Essence without having felt it at least once, we lack the mental image and the desire to research it.

Moreover, we cannot even know ourselves, our own Essence. Perceiving myself as an object that occupies a place, a form, temperature, and ability to think, *I perceive the results of my Essence's actions*, not the Essence itself. We receive the most complete idea in our world with the first kind of attainment—Matter. This information is quite sufficient for our existence and interaction with the surrounding world.

We receive the second kind of attainment, Form in Matter, after researching the surrounding nature using our senses. The evolution of this kind of attainment has led to the creation of science, on which we so deeply rely in every situation in life. This level of attainment of the world is also quite sufficient for humans.

The third kind of attainment, Abstract Form, would have been possible if we could observe this form while detached from matter, rather than while dressed in matter. However, a form can be separated from matter only in imagination (for example, deceitfulness as an abstract notion that is disconnected from a person).

Yet, as a rule, researching a form that is disconnected from matter, in its abstract form, yields no reliable results, and is not confirmed *de facto*. This is even truer when researching forms that have never been dressed in matter!

Thus, we see that of the four kinds of attainment of an object, its Essence is totally imperceptible, and its Abstract Form is attained incorrectly. Only matter and its form, when analyzed in conjunction with matter, yield true and sufficient data about the researched object.

In the spiritual worlds *BYA* every object is attained only in its matter and form. Colors (red, green, and black) in these worlds constitute matter, and we attain them atop the white background of the world *Atzilut*. Readers studying *The Zohar* should remember the necessity to restrict themselves to the two types of research available to us.

As previously mentioned, all the *Sefirot* are subdivided into four levels of attainment. Thus, *Sefirat Hochma* constitutes the Form, and *Bina, Tifferet,* and *Malchut* constitute the Matter dressed in the Form.

Only *Sefirot Bina, Tifferet, and Malchut* are examined in *The Zohar*. The book does not concern itself with examining the form abstracted from matter, let alone with the Essence—the Creator's part (*Ein Sof*) that animates every part of Creation.

Sefirot Bina, Tifferet, and *Malchut* in the world *Atzilut* are available for our research, whereas *Sefirot Keter* and *Hochma*, even at the end of the world *Assiya* are unavailable to us.

All that exists in each world is divided into four levels: Inanimate, Vegetative, Animate, and Human. These correspond to four levels of desire. Similarly, every object consists of these four sub-levels of desire:

- The aspiration to sustain one's existence corresponds to the inanimate level of development.

- The aspiration to wealth corresponds to the vegetative level of development.

- The aspiration to power, fame, and honor corresponds to the animate level of development.

- And the aspiration to knowledge corresponds to the human level.

Thus, we find that we receive the first kind of desire—for necessities and for animate pleasures—from a level inferior to our own. We satisfy the desires for wealth, power, and honor through other people. The desires for education and knowledge are met through higher objects.

All the spiritual worlds resemble one another, differing only in their levels. In this way, the inanimate, vegetative, animate, and human levels in the world *Beria* project themselves onto the corresponding inanimate, vegetative, animate, and human levels in the world *Yetzira*. In their own turn, these levels of the world *Yetzira* become imprinted in the corresponding levels of the world *Assiya* and so on down to our world.

- The inanimate level in the spiritual worlds is called *Heichalot*;
- The vegetative level is called *Levushim*;
- The animate level is called *Mala'achim*;
- The human level is called "human souls" in a particular world.

The ten *Sefirot* in each world are considered the Creator's parts in it. The human souls in each world are its center and receive their sustenance from the other levels.

Those studying *The Zohar* should constantly bear in mind that all objects are viewed only with regard to their interaction in a given world. All research boils down to the study of the human soul and what comes into contact with it.

Since *The Zohar* studies only souls that are clothed in bodies of this world, *Ein Sof* is also studied only in that respect. In other words, the book researches the influence, program, and desire of *Ein Sof* with regard to us, but not with regard to any other objects in other worlds.

The entire program of Creation from beginning to end is included in *Ein Sof*, and the worlds *Beria*, *Yetzira*, *Assiya*, as well as our world, constitute the actual implementation of this program.

Therefore, all actions in all the worlds are consequences of the execution of the program that was rooted in *Ein Sof*, and from there they descend to the world *Atzilut* and break into distinct sub-programs. They come down in a certain order through the worlds to our world in the form of general governance and individual governance.

Human souls originate in the world *Beria*. This is why, starting with this world, one can research their dependency and connection to *Ein Sof*. The ten *Sefirot* in each world of the worlds *BYA* accordingly receive the program, method, and time allotted for the implementation of each of its parts from the ten *Sefirot* of the world *Atzilut*.

Since in the world *Atzilut*, the plan of Creation exists as a program, the Light of *Ein Sof* that passes through *Atzilut* remains uncolored. All the information we obtain is based on the endless transformations of Light, which reveal the colors of *Beria*, *Yetzira*, and *Assiya* to us.

CHAPTER 10
FROM THE INTRODUCTION TO THE ZOHAR

To understand at least something about the surrounding nature and ourselves, we need to have a clear idea of the purpose of Creation and its final state, as the intermediate states are rather deceptive. Kabbalists assert that the purpose of Creation is to bring the created beings to the ultimate pleasure. For this reason, the Creator created souls, the "will to receive pleasure." And since he wished to completely satiate them with delight, He created a massive will to enjoy, well matched for His will to bestow pleasure.

Thus, the soul is the will to enjoy. In accordance with this desire, the soul receives pleasure from the Creator. The amount of received pleasure can be measured by the degree of desire to receive it.

All that exists is either related to the Creator or to His Creation. Prior to the creation of the will to enjoy, or the souls, only the Creator's will to bestow delight existed. Hence, in line with His desire, the will to bestow delight created an equal amount of the will to enjoy; however, it was opposite in property.

Consequently, the will to enjoy is the only thing that was created and exists besides the Creator. Moreover, this will is the material of all the worlds and all objects that populate them. And the pleasure emanating from the Creator vitalizes and governs it all.

In the spiritual worlds, the discrepancy between properties and desires separates two spiritual objects, moving them away from one another just like two corporeal objects separated by distance. In our world, if two people love and hate the same thing, meaning their predilections coincide, we say that they are close to one another.

If their predilections and views differ, their remoteness is proportionate to the difference between their predilections and views. Affinity between people is determined by "spiritual" closeness, not by physical distance. Those who love each other adhere to each other and merge, while those who hate each other are as spiritually distant as two poles.

The will to receive pleasure: The soul is infinitely remote from the Creator because it is opposite from the Creator's will to bestow pleasure. To mend this remoteness of the souls from the Creator, all the worlds were created and divided into two antagonistic systems: the four Light worlds ABYA opposite the four dark worlds ABYA.

The difference between the system of the Light worlds and the system of the dark worlds lies only in the fact that the distinctive property of the first, light worlds is to bestow delight, and the distinctive property of the second, dark worlds, is to receive delight. In other words, the initial desire to enjoy was split into two parts: one remained the same in its properties (to receive) while the other acquired the attributes of the Creator, i.e., drew closer to Him, merged with Him.

Afterwards, the worlds were transformed down to our corporeal world, meaning to the place where humans exist as "body and soul" systems. The body is the will to receive pleasure that descended unchanged through the dark worlds ABYA, which is the will to enjoy for its own sake—egoism.

Hence, a person is born an egoist and continues to exist under the influence of this system until he or she begins to observe the spiritual laws and brings joy to the Creator. In so doing, one gradually purifies oneself of egoism (the will to enjoy for oneself) and acquires the desire to enjoy for the Creator's sake. Then, the soul descends through the whole system of Light worlds and dresses in a body.

Here begins a correction period that continues until all egoism is transformed into altruism (the will to enjoy only for the sake of the Creator).

In this way, one's properties become equalized with those of the Creator, because receiving for the sake of another is not considered reception, but bestowal. Since equivalence of properties means merging, or adhesion, a person automatically receives all that was prepared for him or her in the plan of Creation.

The separation of the divinely created egoistic will to enjoy into two parts (the body and the soul) by the systems of *ABYA* lets us transform the egoistic will to enjoy into a will to enjoy for the Creator's sake. In this way, we can both receive all that was prepared for us, according to the plan of Creation, and become worthy of merging with Him.

This is considered the ultimate purpose of Creation. At this degree, the need for the dark system of *ABYA* disappears and ceases to exist. The work destined to take 6,000 years (the time it takes to transform egoism into the will to enjoy for the Creator's sake) is actually carried out by every person during his or her lifetime and by all generations combined. Everyone must continue to reincarnate until the work is completed. The existence of the dark system of *ABYA* is necessary only for the creation of the body, so that by correcting its egoism, one will acquire one's second, divine nature.

However, if egoism (the selfish will to enjoy) is so base, how could it appear in the Creator's thought? The answer is simple: since time does not exist in the spiritual world, the Creation's final state appeared simultaneously with the plan of Creation. This is because in the spiritual worlds, the past, present and future merge in a single whole.

Therefore, the egoistic will to enjoy) and the resultant opposition of properties and detachment from the Creator have never existed in the spiritual world. From the beginning of Creation to its end, the soul passes through three states. The first state is final; it already exists beside the Creator due to the similarity of properties.

The second state is our reality, where egoism (divided into the body and the soul by the two *ABYA* systems) is transformed into altruism during 6,000 years. During this period, only souls undergo correction. Egoism, inherent in them under the influence of the body, is destroyed and altruism, inherent in them by nature, is acquired.

Even the souls of the righteous do not reach *Gan Eden* (The Garden of Eden—a certain level in the system of the Light Worlds ABYA) until all egoism is destroyed and they rot in the "earth" (*Malchut* of the world *Assiya*).

The third state is the state of the corrected souls after the "revival of the dead," after the correction of the "bodies." It is the situation when egoism, inherent in the body, turns into altruism and the body becomes worthy of receiving all the delight that the Creator had prepared for it. At the same time, the body merges with the Creator because of the equivalence of their qualities. By so doing, it pleases the Creator because unification with the Creator *is the actual* pleasure.

By looking closely at these three states, we will discover that each of them necessitates the emergence of the other. At the same time, the exclusion of one of them will result in the annulment of the others.

For example, if the final, third state had not appeared, the first state would not have appeared either. This is because it only came into being because the third state exists, which is already present in the first state. All perfection of the first state is determined by the projection of the future state on the present. Without the existence of the future state, the present state would have been annulled as well. This is so because there is no time in spirituality, only changing situations.

Prior to the beginning of Creation, in the Thought of Creation, the goal was designed as definitive and existing, and this is where Creation started. Thus, the first and the second states are supported by the last and third state. Generally speaking, contrary to our actions in this world, every act in spirituality begins with designating the potential final state, followed by the act of actually attaining it.

Thus, the future necessitates the existence of the present. And if something had disappeared from the second state (the work on self-correction), how would the third, corrected state (necessitating the first one) have appeared? In the same way, the primary state where perfection already exists, thanks to the future third state, necessitates the existence and completion of both the second and the third states.

However, if the third state already exists (albeit not in our sensations) and, according to the Creator's plan, we are obliged to achieve it, then where is our freedom of will?

It appears from the aforesaid that although we are obliged to attain the set goal, there are two ways to do that, or to pass from the first to the third state:

- The first way is voluntary; it includes a conscious observation of rules prescribed by Kabbalah;

- The second is a path of suffering, because suffering can purify the body of egoism, force it to achieve altruism, and thus merge with the Creator.

The only difference between these two paths is that the first is shorter. After all, the second, or the path of suffering, still brings us back to the first one. In any event, everything is interconnected and mutually necessitates all our states, from the beginning of Creation to its end. Because we are corrupted and mean, we must become as perfect as our Creator. Indeed, a perfect One such as He cannot create imperfection.

Now we understand that the body we possess is not our real body. In fact, our true body, perfect and immortal, exists in its first and third states. In our present (second) state, we are deliberately given a base, corrupt, defective, and completely egoistic body that is detached from the Creator by the difference in desires. We received this body specifically for the purpose of correcting it, and receive an immortal body in its stead, when we reach the third state. Only in our present state can we complete the work.

However, one may say that in the second state, we also exist in absolute perfection. This is because our body (the will to enjoy, egoism), which dies more with every passing day, does not create obstacles for us to reach the desired state. There is only one: the time required for its final elimination and the reception of an eternal, perfect body in its stead, namely the altruistic desire.

Yet, how could such an imperfect universe, namely we and our society with its base inclinations, emerge from such a perfect Creator? The answer is: our transient body, the entire universe, and humanity in its present form were not included in the Creator's purpose. He considers that we already exist in our final state. All that is temporary (such as the body with its egoism) merely facilitates our spiritual ascent by working on ourselves.

All the other created beings populating this world spiritually ascend and descend along with us, and along with us they attain perfection. Since the third state affects the first, we are destined to achieve the set goal by two means: voluntary spiritual development or undergoing suffering, which affects only our bodies.

It follows that egoism was created only to exterminate it from the world and transform it into altruism. Suffering shows us how insignificant the body is to reveal its transience and worthlessness.

When everyone in the world decides to eradicate egoism and think about each other and not themselves, all worries will disappear and everyone will surely live a calm, healthy, and happy life, because everyone will be confident that their well-being will be assured.

But as long as we are stuck in egoism, there is no salvation from the suffering that constantly befalls humanity. On the contrary, the Creator sends these sufferings with the purpose of leading us to decide to choose the path offered by Kabbalah, the path of love and care for one another.

Therefore, Kabbalah considers the instructions that refer to interpersonal relationships to be more important than our duties regarding the Creator. This is because social duties lead to a faster extermination of egoism.

Although we have not yet reached the third state, this in no way belittles us, because it is merely a question of time. We can already feel the future now, in our present state, yet our ability to sense the future depends on our confidence in it. As a result, an absolutely confident person can develop a clear sensation of the third state. When this happens, it is as if our bodies do not exist.

However, the soul exists eternally because this attribute coincides with the Creator (in contrast to the mind, which is the product of matter). The soul acquires the Creator's attribute in the process of development, although its initial nature consists of a will to receive pleasure.

Desire creates needs, and the needs stimulate the appropriate thoughts and knowledge to meet these needs. Since people have different desires, it is only natural that their needs, thoughts, and development will differ.

Those who have only base needs will direct their thoughts and education to satisfying those desires. Although they do use their knowledge and intellect, these are serving the low (animate) mind. People whose ego-based desire for pleasure is limited to such human needs as power over others, use their strength, intellect, and education to satisfy it.

Others' desire to enjoy is focused on using knowledge to receive pleasure. These people must use their minds to fulfill such needs. These three types of desires never occur in their pure forms because they are mixed in various attributes in all of us. It is this combination of desires makes people different.

While passing through the pure (Light) worlds *ABYA*, human souls acquire the ability to receive pleasure for the sake of both others and the Creator. When the soul enters the body, the desire is born for altruism, an aspiration for the Creator. The force of this aspiration will depend on the magnitude of desire.

All that the soul attains in the second state remains in its possession forever, regardless of the degree of decay or age of the body. Conversely, outside of it, the soul instantly receives a corresponding spiritual level and returns to its Root. Naturally, the soul's eternity in no way depends on the knowledge that was acquired during life, which disappeared with the demise of the body. Its eternity lies only in the acquisition of the Creator's traits.

It is known that during the 6,000 years we were given for correction with the help of Kabbalah, we are to correct not our bodies, with their corrupted desire to enjoy, but only our souls, elevating them along the levels of purity and spiritual development. However, the final correction of egoism is possible only in the state called the "revival of the dead."

As previously mentioned, the first state necessitates the existence of the third state to fully manifest. Therefore, the first state requires the "revival of the dead bodies," i.e. the revival of egoism with all its defects. Then, the work to turn egoism in its corrupted form into altruism in the same degree starts anew. This way, we gain twofold:

- We receive an enormous desire to enjoy from the body;

- We enjoy not for ourselves, but for the sake of fulfilling the Creator's desire. It is as though we do not receive pleasure, but rather allow Him to bestow it upon us. As we are similar to Him in action, we are merged with the Creator. He gives us pleasure, and we allow Him to do that; thus, the "revival of the dead" ensues from the first state.

As we now understand, the "revival of the dead" should occur at the end of the second state, after the extermination of egoism, the acquisition of altruism, and the attainment of the soul's highest spiritual level. In this state, the soul achieves perfection and enables the body to experience a revival and complete correction.

By the way, this principle (the "revival of the dead") is effective in every case. When we want to correct a bad habit, attribute, or inclination, we must completely get rid of it. Only then we can resume using it partially in the proper direction. However, until we rid ourselves of it entirely, this habit cannot be used in a proper, intelligent, and independent way. Thus, we can now understand our role in the long chain of reality, where each of us is a tiny link.

Our lives are divided into four periods:

1. The attainment of the maximum level of egoism. We receive this from the dark system of *ABYA* in order to subsequently correct it. The pleasures that we receive in the dark system of *ABYA* will not satisfy the will to enjoy, but will merely increase it.

For example, when one wishes to enjoy and receives pleasure, the desire doubles. When the doubled desire is satisfied, it quadruples. If we do not restrict ourselves from needless desires (using the Kabbalistic method) and cleansing them, and then turning to altruism, our desire will keep growing all through life. Finally, at our deathbed, we discover that we failed to achieve even half of what we wanted.

In other words, although the role of the dark forces is to provide us with material to work on, it usually turns out that we ourselves are the material for the dark forces.

2. In the second period, the pure point in our hearts (which has existed since we were born spiritually) receives power and an opportunity to ascend by observing the spiritual laws with the help of the Light worlds *ABYA*.

The main task in this period is to acquire and increase the desire for maximum spiritual pleasures. At the moment of birth, we desire only material things: to dominate the entire world and seize wealth, fame, and power, in spite of their transience and instability.

However, when we develop the spiritual desire, we want to control the spiritual, eternal world as well. This is both the true desire and the ultimate egoism. By working on oneself, on this enormous will to receive pleasure for self-gratification, we can attain spiritual heights in proportion to our corrected egoism.

Egoism creates tremendous difficulties and pushes us away from the spiritual. Unless continuously and fiercely struggling with ourselves, we begin wishing for everything in the world. If we succeed in the struggle, we feel an unusually strong attraction to the Creator, which helps us merge with Him.

This struggle is not against the desires that we are familiar with in this world, by which one limits and disciplines oneself in using his or her desires. Rather, we cultivate a compelling yearning to attain spirituality and eternity after contemplating the greatness of spirituality, eternity, and domination beyond universe and time. This desire to merge with the Creator is the last level of the second period.

The third period of development includes the study of Kabbalah and observance of the laws of the Upper World. In this, we are assisted by an anti-egoistic screen whose intention is to bring joy to the Creator, and by no means for us to receive for our own benefit. This work corrects and transforms egoism into the desire to perform good deeds, as does the Creator.

In proportion to the annulled part of the egoism, we receive a soul of a certain level, a certain amount of Light and pleasure consisting of five parts: *Nefesh, Ruach, Neshama, Haya, Yechida* (NRNHY). As long as we retain the egoistic will to enjoy, egoism, we will remain detached from the Creator, and even the tiniest particle of the soul cannot enter into our bodies.

However, after completely destroying the ego and attaining the will to enjoy only for the sake of the Creator (by becoming similar to Him), our entire soul (a part of the common soul) immediately takes us over.

The fourth period follows the "revival of the dead," when its complete restoration occurs once the egoism is completely annulled. The work transforming it into altruism resumes, though only a few people in our world can complete this task.

Kabbalah says that all the worlds were created for man's sake (man in the sense of "collective humanity"). However, isn't it strange that the Creator troubled Himself to create all this for such a small object as man, who is lost even in our world, let alone in other worlds? Why does humanity need all of this Creation?

The Creator's enjoyment, which lies in delighting His creatures, depends on how much they can perceive and discern. It also is affected by how much we can discern Him as the giver of all goodness. Only in this case does He receive pleasure from us. This is much like a parent who plays with his or her beloved child and enjoys the child's attitude toward him or her. The parent is delighted that the child recognizes the parent as a loving and strong parent who only awaits the child's requests and is ready to grant them.

Now try to imagine what an immense delight the Creator derives from those perfect ones who rose so high, they recognize and experience all that He had prepared for them. They established a relationship with the Creator resembling that of the parent and the loving and beloved child. From this, you will realize that it was worthwhile for Him to create all the worlds, and the chosen ones will understand even more what those who approach the Creator reveal.

To prepare His created beings for the revelation of the worlds, the Creator gave us four levels of development: inanimate, vegetative, animate, and human, corresponding to the four levels of the will to receive pleasure. The main level is the fourth, but it is attainable only by gradual development, after we have completely mastered each level.

The first level (inanimate) is the beginning of manifestation, the conception of desire in our corporeal world. Its force includes all types of inanimate nature, but none of the elements that form this nature (for example, rocks) can independently move.

The will to enjoy brings forth needs, and these generate movement towards attaining the desired object. In this case (the first level) the will to enjoy is very small. It therefore affects only the sum of all the elements, and is not separately manifested in each of the inanimate elements of nature.

At the next level (vegetative), the will to enjoy is bigger, and already manifests in each particular element. Hence, each element at the vegetative level already possesses the ability for individual movement (for example, plants open their petals and turn toward the sun). This level includes such processes as absorption and excretion, yet beings at this level still lack the sensation of individual freedom of will.

At the third level (animate), the will to receive pleasure grows even larger. Desire produces individual sensations in each particular element and creates a unique life for everyone, one that differs from those of the others. However, there is no sense of empathy with others at this level. These beings still lack the necessary compassion or joy with regard to others.

At the last, fourth level (human), the will to enjoy creates the sensation of others. For example, the difference between the third and the fourth levels is similar to the difference between all the animals put together and a single human being. This is because animals cannot sense others and can generate needs only within the limits of their own desires.

At the same time, a person who can sense another acquires the other's needs, and thus becomes envious of others and wants more and more, until eventually that person desires the entire world.

The Creator's goal is to please the created beings so that they will reveal His greatness and receive all the delight that He had prepared for them. Clearly, only human beings can fulfill this role. Only humans have the necessary sensation of others, and only humans can turn the will to enjoy into a will to please others by following the suggestions of Kabbalah in the process of working on themselves.

The presence of such abilities brings one the sensation of the spiritual worlds and the Creator. By attaining a certain level of NRN-HY (Lights) in a particular spiritual world, a person receives pleasure in accordance with the purpose of Creation.

We may seem small and inconsequential, but it is still man that constitutes the center and the goal of Creation. We are like the worm that lives inside the radish, believing that the whole world is as bitter and small as the radish it was born in. However, when it breaks through the shell of the radish and looks outside, it calls out in amazement: "I thought the whole world was like my radish! Now I see how vast and beautiful the world really is!"

In the same way, we who were born within the shell of egoism and wished only to please ourselves cannot break through this shell without Kabbalah, the instrument of our correction. We cannot turn the will to enjoy into a will to please others and the Creator. This is why we think that the entire world is only what we see and feel, failing to perceive how much good the Creator has prepared for us.

All that was created is divided into five worlds: *Adam Kadmon*, *Atzilut*, *Beria*, *Yetzira*, and *Assiya*. Nevertheless, every one of them consists of an endless number of elements. The five worlds correspond to five *Sefirot*: *Adam Kadmon* corresponds to *Sefirat Keter*, *Atzilut* corresponds to *Sefirat Hochma*, *Beria* to *Sefirat Bina*, *Yetzira* to *Sefirat Tifferet*, and *Assiya* corresponds to *Sefirat Malchut*.

The Light (pleasure) that fills the worlds is accordingly divided into five types: *Yechida, Haya, Neshama, Ruach,* and *Nefesh* (the abbreviation in the reverse order forms the word NRNHY).

Therefore, the world *Adam Kadmon* is filled with pleasure (Light) called *Yechida;* the world *Atzilut* is filled with pleasure called *Haya;* the world *Beria* is filled with pleasure called *Neshama;* the world *Yetzira* is filled with pleasure called *Ruach;* and the world *Assiya* is filled with pleasure called *Nefesh* (see Table 1).

World	Primary Light in Each World	*Sefirot* in Each World (primary *Sefira* in bold) and the Lights that Fill Them
Adam Kadmon	Yechida	**Keter (Yechida)** Hochma (Haya) Bina (Neshama) Tifferet (Ruach) Malchut (Nefesh)
Atzilut	Haya	Keter (Yechida) **Hochma (Haya)** Bina (Neshama) Tifferet (Ruach) Malchut (Nefesh)
Beria	Neshama	Keter (Yechida) Hochma (Haya) **Bina (Neshama)** Tifferet (Ruach) Malchut (Nefesh)
Yetzira	Ruach	Keter (Yechida) Hochma (Haya) Bina (Neshama) **Tifferet (Ruach)** Malchut (Nefesh)
Assiya	Nefesh	Keter (Yechida) Hochma (Haya) Bina (Neshama) Tifferet (Ruach) **Malchut (Nefesh)**

Table 1

From the Creator come the worlds. That is, both the desire to receive delight and the delight that fills them come from the Creator. Yet, each world is in turn divided into *Sefirot*: *Keter, Hochma, Bina, Tifferet,* and *Malchut,* which are filled with their corresponding Lights *NRNHY* (see Table 1)

In addition, there are four levels in each world: Inanimate, Vegetative, Animate, and Human. Palaces (*Heichalot*) correspond to the Inanimate level; robes (*Levushim*) correspond to the Vegetative level; angels (*Mala'achim*) correspond to the Animate level, and human souls (*Neshama*) correspond to the Human level.

These levels are located one inside the other like concentric circles (or onion layers).

- The innermost *Sefirat Keter* influences a particular world as the Creator.

- *Neshamot* (the souls of people who exist in a particular world) dress it.

- Then, *Mala'achim, Levushim,* and *Heichalot* dress one another.

The inanimate, vegetative, and animate levels are created for the sake of the fourth level of desire: the human soul. Therefore, it is as though they dress the human soul (serve it) from the outside. From birth, we possess a part of the common (original) soul. This part is a point in our hearts, within our desires, or egoism. All of Creation is built so that the general laws ruling at every level and in every world manifest in every part of Creation, even the smallest particles.

For example, all that exists is divided into five worlds, or *Sefirot*: *Keter, Hochma, Bina, Tifferet,* and *Malchut.* Each particular world consists of five *Sefirot*, within which even the least significant object is also divided into five *Sefirot.*

As was already mentioned, there are four levels in our world: inanimate, vegetative, animate, and human. These correspond to *Sefirot Malchut, Tifferet, Bina, Hochma*, and their root, *Keter*.

Additionally, every part of the inanimate, vegetative, animate, and human levels is divided into four sub-levels (inanimate, vegetative, animate, and human) according to the magnitude of the desire. Thus, a human desire also consists of four levels: inanimate, vegetative, animate, and human, with the point of the soul at the center of each level.

However, even if one begins to observe spiritual laws without having a special attitude toward the Creator as the ruler of all existence (without due respect and awe because one cannot feel Him), if one wants to receive pleasure only for oneself, yet aspires to acquire an inclination for altruism, this is enough for the point in the heart begin to develop and be felt.

This is what makes Kabbalah and its method of observing spiritual laws so amazing. Hence, study and observance of its principles, despite the egoistic purpose of spiritual growth, will purify and gradually elevate the student, although only up to the first, inanimate level.

To the extent that we elevate the spiritual above the physical and aspire to altruism, we change our desires, thus building the entire structure of this first level. The soul then rises and dresses up in *Sefirat Malchut* of the world *Assiya*, and one's entire body senses the corresponding Light (pleasure) at that level. This Light helps to advance further toward higher levels.

Just as the point of the soul's Light of the *Nefesh* level exists in our hearts at the moment of spiritual birth, so does the point of a higher level of *Ruach* of *Assiya* exists within the entire emerging level of *Nefesh* of *Assiya*.

The same occurs at every level: after completely mastering a level, one passes to the point of the next, higher level. This is the only connection between the lower and higher levels, up to the highest. It is through this point that one can advance toward the Creator.

This Light of *Nefesh* of the world *Assiya* is referred to as the "Light of the inanimate level of the world *Assiya*" because it corresponds to the corrected inanimate part of the desire in the body. The actions of such a person in the spiritual world resemble the actions of the inanimate nature in the corporeal world. In both cases, individual movement is absent, and one merely belongs to the all-encompassing general movement of the collective mass of all the inanimate objects and desires.

In correspondence to the 613 spiritual laws, the object called *Nefesh* of the world *Assiya* includes individual elements resembling 613 organs of the human body. Each of them has a unique perception (pleasure) of the Creator's Light. However, the differences among the parts remain inconspicuous and the Kabbalist perceives only the Light's general impact that spreads equally to all parts. Although there is no difference between the *Sefirot* from the highest (*Keter* of AK) to the lowest (*Malchut* of *Assiya*), such a difference does exist with respect to the person receiving the Light.

Sefirot are divided into vessels and the Light that fills them. The Light emanates from the Creator Himself. The vessels are also called *Sefirot Keter, Hochma, Bina, Tifferet*, and *Malchut*. In the last three worlds, *Beria, Yetzira*, and *Assiya*, these vessels constitute filters that block and precisely measure portions of Light to the receiver.

In this way, everyone receives a portion that exactly corresponds to that soul's spiritual level of development. Although the Light inside them is homogeneous, from the perspective of the receiver, we refer to the Lights as NRNHY because the Light is divided according to the properties of the filters (vessels).

Malchut is the densest filter. The Light received from it is small and is meant only to correct the Inanimate part of the body; hence it is called "the Light of *Nefesh*."

Tifferet is a more transparent filter than *Malchut*; therefore, the portion of Light that it passes from the Creator to us is intended to spiritualize the Vegetative part of the body. It is more intense than the Light of *Nefesh* and is called *Ruach*.

Bina is more transparent than *Tifferet*. It passes on the Creator's Light that is meant to correct the Animate part of the body and is called *Neshama*.

Hochma is the most transparent filter. It passes on the Light to elevate the desires of the Human level. It is called "the Light of *Haya*" and its power is unlimited.

As already pointed out, if we have already attained the level of *Nefesh* (with the help of Kabbalah), the point of the next level, *Ruach*, already exists within us. If we continue applying the method of Kabbalah to fulfill the spiritual laws, we will acquire the Vegetative level of the will to enjoy, which rises and dresses *Sefirat Tifferet of Assiya*. This provides a more powerful Light—*Ruach*—corresponding to the Vegetative level of the body.

Just as plants in our world, compared to the inanimate, are capable of personal movement, a person at the beginning of the spiritual development experiences the awakening of spiritual movements and spiritual forces. Also, as one completely attains the level of *Ruach*, the point of the next level of *Neshama* already exists within that person.

By studying the secrets of Kabbalah, one spiritualizes the animate level in one's desire. When building the entire vessel, one rises and dresses *Sefirat Bina of Assiya* and receives the Light of *Neshama* from it. In this case, a person is called a "pure animal" (cleansed animal), because of the purified animate part of the body.

Just like an animal, such a person acquires an individual sensation of each of the 613 desires, because just like an animal in our world, that person individually makes every movement. The Light that such a person receives differs as much as animals differ from plants in our world.

Upon completely mastering the 613 desires (vessel parts) and receiving a special Light of pleasure for each of its 613 parts, one continues working on oneself. The same Light is used to purify the human part of the desire, which originated from the point that appeared after the vessel of *Neshama* had been completely built.

Once having completed the creation of the corresponding desire at the human level, we can acquire the ability to feel other people's feelings, and to know others' thoughts. The received Light (pleasure) differs from that of the previous level just as a person in our world differs from an animal.

Yet, these five levels are merely the pleasures of NRNHY of the world *Assiya*, i.e. *Nefesh*. Even *Ruach* is absent in it because *Ruach* is the Light in the world *Yetzira*, *Neshama*–in the world *Beria*, *Haya*–in the world *Atzilut*, and *Yechida*–in the world *Adam Kadmon*. However, that which exists in the general is also present in each part of the general, meaning in the specific parts. In other words, these five types of Light are in the world *Assiya*, albeit at the smallest, inanimate level of *Nefesh*.

In the world *Yetzira* these five types of Light exist at the general level of *Ruach*. In the world of *Beria*–it is the NRNHY of the level of *Neshama*; in the world *Atzilut*–it is the NRNHY of the level of *Haya*, and in the world of *Adam Kadmon*, it is the NRNHY of the level of *Yechida*. The difference between the worlds is like the difference between the levels of NRNHY in the world *Assiya*.

Thus, everything depends on the spiritual level of those who wish to attain the Upper World, and therefore equalize their spiritual qualities to the properties of the worlds. Consequently, they become an integral part of the worlds, which explains why all the worlds were created, and why we need them.

Indeed, we would have been unable to attain the Creator without consistently ascending the NRNHY levels of each world. By attaining a certain level, we feel the Light (pleasure) and this helps us continue eradicating the egoistic will to enjoy until we achieve the purpose of Creation—equivalence and adhesion with the Creator.

It is important to understand that the NRNHY constitutes the division of the entire Creation into five parts. That which functions in the general system also functions in its tiniest part. Thus, even the lowest level of the world Assiya consists of its five constituent elements, its individual NRNHY. This is because every infinitesimal desire consists of five parts: Keter (the Creator's representative), Hochma, Bina, Tifferet, and Malchut (the four levels of Creation itself). Additionally, the pleasure guiding it also consists of five types of the Light of NRNHY.

It follows that even the Light of the spiritually inanimate level in the world Assiya cannot be reached without these four kinds of attainment. No one can be dismissed from studying Kabbalah and observing the spiritual laws by means of thought for the good of people and the Creator. No one, either, can attain the level of Ruach or the level of Neshama without studying the secrets of Kabbalah.

Our generation is still immersed in darkness. However, the reason for this is clearly the general decline of faith, and particularly the decline of faith in the wisdom of the sages. The most obvious example of this decline is today's books on Kabbalah, which are teeming with materialized descriptions.

Hence, a need arose for a complete commentary on The Book of Zohar, a work that would save us from misinterpreting Kabbalah. This commentary is called The Sulam (The Ladder) because it helps students gradually climb its rungs and reach spiritual heights. Everything depends on one's desire to attain the depths of the worlds' creation and one's place within them.

The purpose of Kabbalah can be illustrated by the following parable:

A subject in a distant Kingdom broke the law, and by the King's order he was banished from the land. He parted from his friends, family, and all that was dear to him. At first he was very sad in his new location, but gradually, as with all things in life, he got used to his new home and completely forgot where he had been born and how he had once lived. He remembered neither that he was exiled, nor that he had ever lived elsewhere. He built a house, made new friends, and built a life. One day, he found a book about his home Kingdom. He remembered where it was and what a wonderful life he had had there. After contemplating the book, he understood why he had been exiled and how he could return there.

That Kingdom is the spiritual world, where everything is fine for those who observe the laws of the Great King. The land of exile is our world. The book through which everyone can remember the forgotten, find the homeland of the soul, realize why he or she had been expelled, and finally return to the original place, is *The Zohar*!

Yet, if *The Zohar* is so important that it can help us attain the Upper Worlds, to see and feel the world of souls and the Creator Himself, why was it concealed for so many years–from the time it was written until the appearance of the Ari's Kabbalistic method?

The answer to this question is found in Kabbalah: for 6,000 years of its existence, the world has been structured as ten *Sefirot*, where *Keter* designates the Creator's influence and the other *Sefirot* are divided into three groups (see below and in Drawing 3 on next page):

- Head: *Hochma, Bina, Daat*;
- Middle: *Hesed, Gevura, Tifferet*;
- End: *Netzah, Hod, Yesod*.

The 6,000 years are also divided into three parts:

- 2,000 years – darkness;
- 2,000 years – the preparation period; and
- 2,000 years – the days of the *Messiah* (Redeemer).

```
Keter ——— The Creator's Influence
Hochma  ⎫
Bina    ⎬  Darkness
Daat    ⎭  0 - 2,000 (Head)
Hesed   ⎫
Gevura  ⎬  Preparation Period
Tifferet⎭  2,000 - 4,000 (Head)
Netzah  ⎫
Hod     ⎬  Days of the Messiah
Yesod   ⎭  2,000 - 4,000 (Head)
```

Drawing 3

The first 2,000 years refer to the head, meaning this period receives the small Light (*Nefesh*) because the *Sefirot* are inversely related to the Creator's Light that fills them. The first group (higher *Sefirot*) appears first: *Hochma, Bina, Daat*, albeit these are filled with a small Light. This first 2,000-year period is called "the darkness period."

During the second 2,000 years, when the second group of *Sefirot* (*Hesed, Gevura,* and *Tifferet*) develops, the Light of *Nefesh* that filled the first group of *Sefirot* descends to the second one, and the Light of *Ruach* fills the first group. These 2,000 years, following the darkness period, are called "the Torah period."

The third group of *Sefirot, Netzah, Hod,* and *Yesod*, takes the last 2,000 years. The Light of *Nefesh* descends here from the second group, the Light of *Ruach* descends from the first group to the second, and the Light of *Neshama* enters the first group.

The entire wisdom of Kabbalah, and *The Zohar* in particular, was concealed until the emergence of the third group. The Ari revealed *The Zohar* to us, and his commentaries showed us the path to attain the spiritual world. The Ari passed away before the end of that period, meaning before all the Light had entered the third group. Hence, at that time only special souls could study Kabbalah without revealing its essence to the world. Today, as we are approaching the end of the third period, we are ready to receive the comprehensive

Sulam (Ladder) commentary on *The Zohar*, and a systematic textbook on Kabbalah entitled *Talmud Eser Sefirot (The Study of the Ten Sefirot).*

Although the souls who lived during the first and the second 2,000 years were highly exalted and corresponded to the upper *Sefirot* (*Hochma, Bina, and Daat, Netzah, Gevura, and Hod*), they could not receive the appropriate Light because it had not yet reached our world. Now, the lowest souls are descending to our world, as the events in our world testify, yet these souls are the ones that complete the structure. The Upper Light enters the upper souls that have already ascended from our world to the Upper Worlds, whose Light reaches us as Surrounding Light.

Although the souls of the first generations exceeded ours in quality, because the pure souls were first to appear in our world, the science of Kabbalah, its inner, concealed part (as well as other sciences) is being revealed only in the latest generations, since it depends on the intensity of the Light.

The lower the souls, the bigger the Light that is revealed and enters our world. This is because a lower Light can descend from the upper to the lower *Sefirot* (or souls) and the Upper Light enters the emptied spaces in the Upper *Sefirot* (souls).

The fulfillment of the correction refers to *Sefirot* (souls), and mental observance (intention) refers to the Light entering the souls. The same reverse dependence exists between the *Sefirot* (souls) and the Light: the Creation starts with the upper *Sefirot*, filled with the lower Lights, and ends with the lower *Sefirot* (souls), filled with the Upper Light. Thus, it is the low souls that reveal the Upper Light, but only if they engage in the proper study of Kabbalah.

The study of *The Zohar*, and Kabbalah itself, is a starting point in the correction of the entire world and the achievement of absolute peace and happiness.

CHAPTER 11
FROM THE INTRODUCTION TO THE STUDY OF THE TEN SEFIROT

In the *Introduction to the Study of the Ten Sefirot*, Baal HaSulam (Rabbi Yehuda Ashlag) explains that his principal desire is to break the iron wall that has been separating us from Kabbalah and prevent the disappearance of this science from our world once and for all. However, many objections have been raised against the study of Kabbalah, all of which stem from ignorance concerning its essence and purpose.

Baal HaSulam continues to explain that if we ask ourselves, "What is the meaning of our lives, these numbered, bitter, hard years that are full of troubles? Who can enjoy it? What does the Creator demand of us?" where are the answers to these questions?

Finally, he states that Kabbalah asserts the following: "Taste and see that the Lord is good" (referring to the sensing of the Creator acquired through the study of Kabbalah). You will see that He is absolutely kind that He created it all for our benefit, and gave us Kabbalah to attain it. You will feel it all while living here in this world. Kabbalah encourages us to "Choose life," to choose goodness, not death, meaning a bitter and meaningless existence. It is said, "Choose," which means that we are given a choice.

It has been clarified in previous articles that choice pertains only to that between two paths to attain the preordained goal: there is the path of spiritual development (the path of Kabbalah) or the path of suffering. The final goal is to eradicate egoism and to acquire a nature of love and bestowal.

How can this be achieved? It is written, "Sleep on the ground, be content with only bread and water, and you will be happy in this world and in the next world." This way one can acquire the spiritual nature, merge with the Upper Worlds, and only afterwards feel the Creator's goodness.

However, only special individuals (souls) can attain the goal this way. Therefore, another path has been granted us: the study of Kabbalah. Its Light affects the soul and transforms it in the right direction. In so doing, we tread a path of attainment through the heart and mind, not through physical sufferings.

However, the Light of Kabbalah influences only those who are loyal and faithful to the Creator, those who believe in His good deeds. The principal requirement for being on this path is faith in the Creator, measured by the time and effort one devotes to this.

Thus, the task boils down to achieving the utmost confidence in the Creator's strength, protection, and love for those who are advancing towards Him. This faith cannot be acquired from any other source except through the study of Kabbalah. The principal strength of Kabbalah lies in the fact that it directly studies the Creator's actions. Hence, the Upper Light that comes from it is intense and quickly corrects us.

The wisdom of Kabbalah consists of two parts: a secret part that has never been described and is passed orally; and a revealed part that was explained in many books. One should study the revealed part because attaining the goal depends solely on it.

The Upper Light's influence is positive only when the goal of a Kabbalah student is to eradicate personal egoism and merge with the Creator. One cannot instantly attune to the desired goal; it must be constantly pursued while studying. This is particularly true by studying the spiritual worlds and the Creator's actions. In this way, students find it easier to concentrate on the thoughts and the desire to merge with what is being studied.

Our remoteness from the spiritual world is the cause of all pain, trouble, suffering, and futility. Our own misunderstanding of how the world is ruled, and our inability to sense the Creator lead us to incomprehension of His governance. Indeed, if the world's governance were revealed, if reward and punishment immediately followed our actions, everyone would be righteous!

Thus, the only thing we lack is a tangible perception of the governance. This concrete attainment unfolds in four stages:

- A double concealment of the Creator's actions;
- A single concealment;
- Attainment of cause and effect, reward and punishment;
- Absolute attainment, once it becomes clear that everything was created for the good of all created beings, both good and bad.

The Creator is actually doubly concealed from human beings in their initial state. In this state, one sees no consequences of the Creator's presence in the world and believes in nature. A single concealment is a state when misfortunes befall the person due to insufficient closeness to the Creator. Human beings in this state believe that they are the result of personal actions, as well as the Creator's governance. This concealment is where one believes in the presence of the Upper Governance.

These two concealments constitute the principal work of approaching the Creator, because due to the Creator's concealment, freedom of will becomes possible. As one advances toward the Creator in faith, while aspiring to see Him in every action, the Creator gradually reveals Himself. In that state, the person clearly sees all the causes and effects of the world's governance, and eradicates egoism once recognizing the need for it and its enormous benefits. Naturally, at this point, one cannot turn back because one feels and foresees punishment.

While continuing to purify, one achieves the level of absolute love for the Creator and thus acquires absolute attainment of Him. This is the ultimate goal of every individual. All the worlds and the forces that control and populate them were created for this purpose.

It is written, "Attain your world and see it while you are still alive." This is the reward for a long and difficult path in darkness, in a state where the Creator is concealed, and when we use our willpower in defiance of nature and society, overcoming the barrier between our world and the spiritual one in search of the Creator. The more obstacles and the greater the distance we must traverse, the stronger the attained sensation of mutual love.

This goal should be constantly pursued in the study of Kabbalah, for only then can we succeed. Otherwise, this study will turn against us and only increase our egoism. This is why it is so important for those of us who are so remote from the Creator to study Kabbalah, which describes the Creator's actions, thoughts, and goals. It helps us to know Him better, and through this knowledge, we will come to love Him and aspire to Him. Although we all start from the farthest point, everyone is obliged to achieve the level of love and complete attainment of the Creator.

Before being handed to us, Kabbalah had passed through a great number of consecutive restrictions from the level of its creation in the world *Atzilut*. However, its essence is constant and unchanging. The lower the level of the created beings, the more important it becomes for them. It helps them to free themselves from the shackles of a body constrained by its inner desires.

In our world, Kabbalah is hidden under coverings (nature, animate creatures, and time) that are controlled from the world *Atzilut*. These shells are the sources of our suffering because they conceal the system of governance.

The shells and the concealed part of the worlds, *Beria*, *Yetzira*, and *Assiya* are called Kabbalah, and the shell of our world is called "revealed science." Until one enters the shell of the world *Yetzira*, regardless of what is being studied, one deals with the concealed part of Kabbalah. However, upon entering the world *Yetzira*, one reveals Kabbalah and the Light replaces the meaningless names.

Thus, one starts learning Kabbalah from a secret until it becomes a reality. This corresponds to the Creator's double and single concealments in the world *Assiya*, to the revelation in the world *Yetzira*, the attainment of love for the Creator in the world *Beria*, and to the merging in absolute love in the world *Atzilut*. Ari's book, *The Tree of Life*, was written to help people attain the Creator consistently, painlessly, and with confidence.

CHAPTER 12
CONDITIONS FOR DISCLOSING THE SECRETS OF THE WISDOM OF KABBALAH

There are three reasons for the concealment of Kabbalah:

- There is no necessity,
- It is impossible, and
- It is the Creator's personal secret.

In every single detail in Kabbalah, these three prohibitions are simultaneously imposed.

The ban, **no necessity to disclose,** means that the disclosure of the wisdom brings no benefit. The only possible benefit might be the case of an obvious benefit for society. People who live by the principle, "So what?" (I did what I did and there is no harm in it), engage in and force others to engage in details that are utterly unnecessary. They are the source of much suffering in the world. Hence, Kabbalists accepted only those students who could keep it secret and refrain from needlessly disclosing it.

The ban, **impossible to disclose,** stems from limitations of the language that cannot describe subtle spiritual concepts. Since all verbal attempts are doomed to fail and lead to erroneous conclusions that will only confuse the student, the revelation of these secrets requires special permission from Above.

A special permission from above is described in the works of the great Kabbalist, the Ari: "Know that the souls of great Kabbalists are filled with the Outer (Surrounding) Light or with the Inner Light (filling). The souls filled with the Surrounding Light have the gift to expound on the secrets by vesting them in words, so that only the worthy can understand it.

"The soul of the great Kabbalist Rashbi (Rabbi Shimon Bar-Yochai, lived in the 2nd century BCE), the author of *The Book of Zohar,* was filled with the Surrounding Light; hence, he had the power to explain the secrets of the universe in such a way that when he spoke before the Great Assembly, only the worthy understood him. Therefore, he alone received the divine permission to write *The Book of Zohar.* Although Kabbalists who lived before him knew more, they did not have his gift of enrobing spiritual concepts in words."

Thus we see that the conditions for divulging Kabbalah depend not on the knowledge of a Kabbalist, but on the attributes of the Kabbalist's soul. Only because of this does a Kabbalist receive instruction from Above to disclose a certain part of Kabbalah.

That is why we do not find any fundamental works on Kabbalah composed prior to *The Book of Zohar.* Those that are available contain only vague and inconsequential hints. After Rashbi, only the Ari was allowed to reveal another part of Kabbalah. Although Kabbalists who had lived before him probably knew a lot more than he did, they did not receive permission from Above.

The ban, **The Creator's personal secret,** means that Kabbalistic secrets are only revealed to those who are devoted to the Creator and revere Him. This is the most important reason for keeping Kabbalah's secrets from a wide circle of people. Many frauds used Kabbalah in their own interests by luring simpletons with soothsaying, making amulets, "saving" people from the evil eye, and other so-called miracles.

Originally Kabbalah was concealed for this very reason. Therefore, the true Kabbalists committed to subjecting their disciples to very stringent tests. This explains why even the few people in every generation granted permission to study Kabbalah were sworn not to reveal even a small detail of it, which fell under the three above-listed bans.

However, we should not think that these three bans divide Kabbalah into three parts. On the contrary, every part, word, concept, and definition in Kabbalah falls under this division into three types of concealment of the genuine meaning, and it is constantly effective in this science.

The question does arise: if this secret science was so thoroughly concealed, how did all the Kabbalistic compositions appear? The answer is: the first two bans differ from the third, because the last ban is the strictest of all. The first two parts are not permanently valid because, depending on the external social reasons, the condition, **no necessity to disclose,** sometimes turns into the instruction, **There *is* a need to disclose**. With the development of humanity, or due to the received permission (as in the cases of the Ari, Rashbi and, to a lesser extent, other Kabbalists), genuine books on Kabbalah begin to appear.

CHAPTER 13
KEY CONCEPTS

Kabbalah is a method for revealing the Creator to the created beings existing in this world. Kabbalah derives from the word *Lekabel* (to receive). The goal of those who live in this world is to receive all the infinite pleasure for which the entire Creation was formed.

The sensation of another person is developed only in humans. It endows envy, empathy, shame, and the sensation of spiritual ascent. The ability to sense others was created in us to enable us to sense the Creator.

The sensation of the Creator means that everyone feels the Creator in exactly the same way as one feels one's fellow person. It is said that Moses spoke to the Creator "face to face." This means that he had a sense of absolute attainment of the Creator, to the extent of intimacy in his contact with Him, as with a friend.

The end of an action is determined by the original thought: Just like a person who is building a house first makes a plan and works on specifications according to the final goal, all one's actions are determined by the final, predetermined goal.

After clarifying the ultimate goal of Creation, we realize that Creation and the ways to control it correspond to this ultimate goal. The purpose of the governance lies in humanity's gradual development, until we feel the Creator just as we feel other created beings in our world.

From above downward is a path of a gradual attainment of the spiritual. In other words, this is our development to the point where one can feel another exactly as one feels oneself, and feel spiritual objects as clearly as one feels corporeal objects, and so forth at all levels up to the Creator Himself. This is the Creator's order of attainment, which moves along the same levels by which Creation passed on its descent from Above. This means that this path already exists, and as we reveal the higher levels, we completely reveal the corresponding lower levels as well.

From below upward is the order of Creation of both worlds: the spiritual and our final, material one.

The spiritual observance of the laws of Creation: The thought and desire to achieve the purpose of Creation becomes the means to attain spiritual perfection.

The periods in Kabbalah: Since the beginning of Creation and up to the destruction of the Second Temple, Kabbalists have "openly" studied Kabbalah. All spiritual forces were perceived more tangibly in our world, and our contact with the spiritual worlds was closer and more significant, particularly through the Temple and the services conducted there.

As the moral level of society declined, we became unworthy (i.e., different in qualities) and lost our ability to sense the spiritual worlds. Hence, the Temple was destroyed and the exile period began. Kabbalists continued studying secretly and made Kabbalah inaccessible to the "unworthy."

It is written in *The Zohar* that the Creator's desire was to conceal His wisdom from the world, but when the world approaches the days of the Messiah, even children will reveal His secrets. They will be able to foresee and study the future, and at that time He will reveal Himself to all.

Rashbi was the last Kabbalist of the pre-exile period; hence, he received permission from Above to write *The Book of Zohar*.

Kabbalah was forbidden for almost fifteen centuries, until the Kabbalist Ari (Rabbi Yitzhak Luria) appeared and spiritually attained the whole Kabbalah. In his works he revealed *The Zohar* for us: "...in 600 years of the sixth millennium the sources of wisdom will open up above and flow down."

In one of the ancient manuscripts, Kabbalist Abraham Azulai (sixth century CE) found that "from the year 5,300 (1,539 CE) since Creation, everyone will be permitted to openly study Kabbalah, adults and children, and just because of this, the Redeemer shall come."

As a sign that we live at the end of days, the great Kabbalist Yehuda Ashlag (Baal HaSulam) appeared in our time and explicated the whole Kabbalah in a clear and comprehensible language, using a method that is suitable for our souls.

The uniqueness of the science of Kabbalah lies in the fact that it includes complete knowledge about our world (i.e., all sciences in their unrevealed entirety) and its elements, because it studies the roots that control our world, and from which our world appeared.

The soul is an "I" that everyone feels. On closer examination, the soul divides a force into our body, which vitalizes it, creating "the animate" soul, as well as a force of aspiration to the spiritual, known as "the spiritual" (divine) soul, which is practically nonexistent in spiritually undeveloped people.

The physical body and the animate soul are the products of our world. They are sufficient for us to perceive through sense organs. By developing a spiritual soul, we acquire the ability to feel beyond the "I." This occurs when the spiritual, altruistic "I" emerges from the negation of the egoistical "I." Thus, we begin to sense more intense spiritual vibrations until we develop the soul from "a point" up to its intrinsic capacity.

The inner essence of Kabbalah is the research of the Light of the Creator, which emanates from Him and reaches us according to certain laws.

The law of roots and branches is the law that determines the operations of the forces that impel all parts of our world's creation to grow and develop. It is said in Kabbalah: "There is no grain below without its angel above that strikes it and tells it: Grow!" **The language of branches** also helps reveal information about what occurs in other worlds. Creatures that populate a certain world perceive objects in that world in a similar way, and can thus exchange information using their own language. One can inform others about what happens in other worlds using the same language, while at the same time implying that this refers to objects in another world, which correspond to our own. This is exactly the language in which the Torah is written.

All the worlds are similar to one another; the difference is only in the material from which they are created—the higher the world, the "purer" its matter. However, the laws of their functioning and form are the same, and each subsequent world is an exact replica (branch) of its predecessor (root).

The created beings populating a certain world can perceive only within its boundaries because sense organs perceive only the material of that particular world. Only humans can simultaneously attain all the worlds.

The levels of attainment are the consecutive degrees of perception of the Creator. It is as though they form a ladder that climbs from our world to the spiritual worlds. The bottom rung of that ladder is called "the *Machsom*" (barrier). It conceals all the spiritual forces from us so completely that we have no perception of them whatsoever. Hence, we try to find the Source and the purpose of life in our world.

Light in the spiritual worlds: Information, feelings, and pleasures are passed by the expansion and retraction of the spiritual force called "Light" (by analogy with the light in our world that gives life and warmth, or with the light pertaining to thought, clarity, and enlightenment).

The right to exist: Everything in our world, good, bad, even the most harmful, has a right to exist. We are given an opportunity to make corrections and improvements. There is nothing redundant or unnecessary in our world. Everything is created for the good of humanity, both directly and indirectly. Thus, by correcting ourselves, we neutralize any detrimental influences.

Correction: The Creator has not finished creating our world; we are entrusted with the task of completing and perfecting it. We see our world as a fruit that remains bitter during its ripening, and it is our task and goal to correct and sweeten it.

Two paths of correction:

4. The path of acceptance of the spiritual laws of Correction by everyone is called "the path of Light." It is preferable from the Creator's perspective because His goal is to bestow joy to His created beings at all the stages of their existence. Thus, we would not taste the bitterness of the fruit.

5. **The path of suffering:** Through trial and error during a period of 6,000 years, humanity realizes the need to observe the laws of Creation one way or another.

Reward is pleasure (the taste of the ripe fruit). We can only influence ourselves; we cannot influence anything outside of us. Hence, correction can only be made when everyone works on self-perfection.

A Kabbalist is any person in our world who attains similarity to the Creator. By studying and observing the spiritual laws, we develop ourselves spiritually to an extent where we become a part of the spiritual worlds.

Attainment occurs through inner work on ourselves, by studying the nature and attributes of the spiritual objects. We do not speak about psychological sensations, fantasies, or suggestion. What is meant here is a genuine ascent to a world whose substance is spiritual, above and beyond all human psychological perception.

Pleasure can be felt only if desire and aspiration are available. A desire can exist only if the resultant pleasure is known. Aspiration is possible only in the absence of pleasure at a given moment. A person who was not released from prison does not enjoy freedom, and only a sick person can truly appreciate good health. We receive both desires and aspirations from the Creator.

The only created thing is the sensation of deficiency, which is absent in the Creator. The more developed one is, the more keenly one will feel it. This deficiency is rather limited in simple people and children. A true human being wants the entire world. A wise one wants not only our world, but all the other worlds as well.

A combination of desire and aspiration is called a *Kli* (vessel) in Kabbalah. The pleasure itself, *Ohr* (Light), emanates from the Creator.

The sensation of pleasure: The vessel feels the entrance of the Light, depending on the similarity between the qualities of the vessel and those of the Light. The more similar these qualities are, the more the vessel can bestow, love, and bring joy, and the smaller its will to receive. The closer the vessel is to the Light, the more Light and pleasure it feels.

Existence in the spiritual worlds: Our ability to feel or not to feel the Creator (the Light) depends only on our closeness to Him, based on our equivalence of attributes with Him. This is because every one of us is a vessel. As long as the vessel has even the slightest desire to bestow, to think of others, to suffer for them, to love and help them while disregarding its own desires, this vessel exists in the spiritual worlds, and its properties determine which world it will occupy.

The recognition of evil: When the intention to bestow is absent in a vessel, it perceives itself in this world. Such a vessel is called a person's "body," whose only wish is to care for itself. We cannot even imagine the ability to selflessly do something for another. By undergoing "the recognition of evil"—an accurate and rigorous self-analysis—one can determine one's inability to selflessly do for another.

The vessel's perfection: The vessel (*Kli*) is created in such a way that it contains desires for all the pleasures that exist in the Light. Because of the restriction and the breaking of the vessels, a certain number of separate vessels were formed. Each of these vessels moves from one state (world) to another, which leads to separation (death).

While living in this world, everyone must make the attributes of their vessel similar to the Light, receive a corresponding measure of Light, and reunite with the other vessels (souls) to form a single vessel completely filled with Light (pleasure). This future state is called *Gmar Tikkun* (The End of Correction).

The entrance of Light into the vessel: The differences among people are based on the magnitude of their desires. The ban imposed on spiritual coercion and murder is quite clear. By studying the properties of the spiritual vessels, material vessels (human beings) stimulate the desire to be similar to it. And since desire in the spiritual world constitutes action, by gradually changing ourselves, we allow the Light to enter our vessels. While inside the vessel, the Light purifies it because the Light's nature is "to bestow." Through this property, the Light gradually modifies the characteristics of the vessel as well.

The First Restriction (*Tzimtzum Aleph*) is a ban, an oath that the first, collective spiritual vessel imposed on itself immediately after its appearance. It means that although the Creator's sole desire is to fill the vessel with delight, the vessel imposed a condition on itself that it will not enjoy for itself, but only for the Creator.

Thus, only the thought changed, not the action itself. This means that the vessel receives the Light not because it wants it, but because such is the Creator's wish. Hence, our goal is to fulfill the will to receive, to wish for pleasure the way the Creator wishes for it.

Sensation is the attribute of reacting to the absence or presence of the Light, even in its infinitely small portions. In principle, our whole life consists of mere cycles of sensations. Usually, it does not matter to us what we enjoy, but we cannot live without pleasure. Recognition and fame merely provide a sensation, but pleasure is so important to us!

Our state always depends on the mood and perception of our surroundings, regardless of the world's state. None of our sensations is the product of our inner life and the environment's influence, for their source is the Creator Himself, as every sensation constitutes either the Light or its absence.

We feel either ourselves or the Creator or both, depending on our moral state. While feeling only ourselves, we can believe that the Creator exists and influences us. The fact that we perceive ourselves as independent creatures, and even believe that only we exist, is a result of our spiritual disparity from the Creator, and of our remoteness from Him.

Intention (*Kavana*) is the single most important thing in every action that a person makes. This is so because in the spiritual world, a thought constitutes an action. Similarly, in our corporeal world, one who cuts another with a knife intending to inflict harm is punished, while another uses a knife with the aim to heal—as in surgery—and is awarded.

If sentence is passed according to the absolute laws of the spiritual worlds, then for every evil thought a person should be spiritually punished. Indeed, in spirituality this is exactly what happens.

Our mood and our health also depend on our intentions, but not on the difficulty or character of our work or financial state. It should be noted that while we can only control our physical actions, we can only change our feelings through the spiritual world.

This is why prayer is of such paramount importance; it essentially constitutes every appeal (even wordless ones, coming from the heart) to The Source of all that exists, the Creator, for whom all created beings are equal and desired.

CHAPTER 14
FREQUENTLY ASKED QUESTIONS

Question: What is the subject of Kabbalah?

From the beginning of time, humankind has been searching for answers to the principal questions of existence: Who am I? What is the purpose of my life? Why does the world exist, and do we continue to exist after death?

Every person tries to find his or her own answers to these questions from the sources of information at one's disposal. All of us develop our own outlook on the world, guided by the approach that seems most reliable.

The question about the meaning of life adds a more global discontentment to the daily suffering: What am I suffering for? This question does not let us feel content, even when one of our day-to-day desires is temporarily satisfied.

Even when we attain our goal, soon we begin to feel dissatisfaction. Looking back, we see how much time we had spent on achieving the desired object, but received very little pleasure in return.

Since there are no answers to the above questions, people's aspirations turn to ancient faiths. Meditations and physical and psychological practices help us feel more comfortable. But this is just an attempt to forget ourselves, since our desires remain unsatisfied and the meaning of life is still abstruse. All those methods soothe us, not because they provide an answer to the question about the purpose of life and the meaning of suffering, but because it helps us decrease our demands.

However, soon we discover that the truth cannot be ignored. Humanity is constantly seeking a logical reason for its existence; humankind has studied the laws of nature for thousands of years.

Modern scientists realize that the farther they advance in their research, the foggier and more tangled the picture of the world becomes. Modern scientific books resemble works on mysticism and science fiction, yet fail to provide an answer to the question about the meaning of life.

The science of Kabbalah offers its own method of researching the world. It helps us develop the ability to feel the concealed part of the universe. Kabbalists tell us about a technique based on their personal experience. In their books, they teach the method of researching the universe, and show how to receive the answer to the question about the meaning of life.

Question: Why is Kabbalah called a "secret science?"

Kabbalah is the closest science to man because it speaks of the purpose of life, of why we are born and live in this world. Kabbalah explains the meaning of life, where we came from, and where we go once we complete our earthly term.

Kabbalists receive answers to these questions while still living here in this world. The study of Kabbalah provides knowledge about the spiritual worlds and at the same time develops an additional, sixth sense organ, which perceives the surrounding reality. It is in this sense that a person feels the concealed part of the universe.

The attainable, usually concealed, part of the universe gives us all the answers to all the questions we ask about ourselves. Nothing is closer and more important to us than this knowledge, because it teaches us about ourselves, the world we live in, and about our own destiny.

Everything we learn about ourselves and the world, we reveal by ourselves and within ourselves. All this happens while our feelings and accumulating knowledge are concealed from others, which is why Kabbalah is called "the science of the hidden."

Question: Who is a Kabbalist?

A Kabbalist is a person who, on the outside, is like any other person. A Kabbalist does not have to be clever or learned. There is nothing unusual in the outward appearance. They are ordinary people who, through studying Kabbalah, acquired an additional "sixth sense," a sensation of the concealed part of the world. It is concealed from ordinary people, who refer to it as "the spiritual world." A Kabbalist can perceive the entire universe with this newly acquired sense, perceiving both our world and the spiritual world as tangible reality, just as we perceive our everyday reality.

Kabbalists feel the Upper World and directly attain it. It is called "the Upper World" because it exists beyond our ordinary perception. Kabbalists see that everything descends from the Upper World and appears in ours. They see all the causes and effects because they simultaneously exist in both the Upper World and in our world.

An ordinary person perceives only a fraction of the surrounding universe and calls this fraction "our world." A Kabbalist perceives the entire scope of the universe.

Kabbalists pass their knowledge along in books written in a special language. Therefore, one can only study these books under the guidance of a Kabbalist, and by following a special method. In such a case, these books become a means for the attainment of the true reality.

Question: Why is it important to study Kabbalah?

Every person has an opportunity to develop the sixth sense. Kabbalists write their books while perceiving and being under the direct influence of the spiritual worlds. By reading these books, the reader attracts the "Surrounding Light" to him or her self, even without understanding all that is written in them.

While studying, we draw this Light on ourselves, and the Light gradually reveals the complete picture of reality to us. This sixth, spiritual sense, which can perceive the entire universe, is dormant within everyone. It is called "a point in the heart." Only the Surrounding Light is destined to fill it. The Light is called "Surrounding" because it surrounds the sixth sense while still unable to fill it.

This point, the embryo of the sixth sense "expands" and acquires sufficient "volume" to allow the Surrounding Light inside it. The entry of Light into the point in the heart creates in the student the first sensation of the Spiritual, the Divine, the Beyond. As the Light enters the point, we perceive a wider and clearer picture of the Upper World and see our past and future.

In the *Introduction to the Study of the Ten Sefirot*, item 155, it is written:

"Why do Kabbalists obligate each person to study Kabbalah? This is because even when people who study Kabbalah do not understand what they are learning, through their desire to understand they awaken upon themselves the Light that surrounds their souls. This means that every person is guaranteed to attain all that the Creator has prepared in the Thought of Creation. One who has not achieved it in this life will be granted it in one of the next lives. Until one becomes capable of receiving this Light within, it continues to shine outside and wait for that person to create a sense of its perception."

When we are studying Kabbalah, the Surrounding Light instantly shines on us without being dressed within our souls, as the sixth sense has not yet been developed. Nevertheless, the Light that we receive every time during our studies purifies and makes us fit to receive the Light within. The reception of the Light grants absolute knowledge, calm, and the sensation of immortality.

Question: How is the Kabbalistic information conveyed?

Kabbalists have passed on their knowledge about the Upper World both orally and in writing. Initially, it appeared in Mesopotamia in the 18th century BCE. The accumulated knowledge was expounded upon in *The Book of Creation (Sefer Yetzira)*, ascribed to Abraham. This book is still available in bookstores.

In every generation, Kabbalists wrote their books for the souls of that particular generation. Several languages have been used in Kabbalah over the centuries. This is because the development of the human soul occurs gradually. From generation to generation, the increasingly coarser souls return to this world with the experience of past lives. They bring the burden of additional suffering, but also contribute their spiritual "luggage." Although this information is concealed from the individual, it exists in the point of one's heart.

Therefore, to understand Kabbalah, every generation needs its own language, suitable for the descending souls. The development of humanity is a descent of souls to this world. As they descend to our world and manifest in new bodies in every generation, the same souls develop, realize the need for the spiritual advancement, and attain the supernal knowledge, eternity, and perfection.

Question: How long does it take to start feeling the spiritual world?

In the *Introduction to the Study of the Ten Sefirot* it is written that a person who studies by the genuine sources can enter the spiritual world within three to five years. This means that if one studies with the right intention, such a student crosses the barrier between this world and the spiritual world and attains the Upper Light.

FURTHER READING

Attaining the Worlds Beyond: is a first step toward discovering the ultimate fulfillment of spiritual ascent in our lifetime. This book reaches out to all those who are searching for answers, who are seeking a logical and reliable way to understand the world's phenomena. This magnificent introduction to the wisdom of Kabbalah provides a new kind of awareness that enlightens the mind, invigorates the heart, and moves the reader to the depths of their soul.

Awakening to Kabbalah: a distinctive, personal, and awe-filled introduction to an ancient wisdom tradition. Rav Laitman—a disciple of the great Kabbalist Rabbi Baruch Ashlag (son of Yehuda Ashlag)—provides you with a deeper understanding of the fundamental teachings of Kabbalah, and how you can use this wisdom to clarify your relationship with others and the world around you.

Using language both scientific and poetic, he probes the most profound questions of spirituality and existence. This provocative, unique guide will inspire and invigorate you to see beyond the world as it is and the limitations of your everyday life, become closer to the Creator, and reach new depths of the soul.

The Kabbalah Experience: Never has the language of Kabbalah been as clear and accessible as it is here, in this compelling, informative collection. The depth of wisdom revealed in the questions and answers of this book will inspire reflection and contemplation. Readers will also begin to experience a growing sense of enlightenment while simply absorbing the words on every page.

The Kabbalah Experience is a guide from the past to the future, revealing situations that all students of Kabbalah will experience at some point on their journeys. For those who cherish every moment in life, the author offers unparalleled insights into the timeless wisdom of Kabbalah.

The Path of Kabbalah: "Thou shalt not make unto thee a graven image, nor any manner of likeness" (Exodus 20:3). This prohibition from the Bible is also the basis of the Wisdom of Kabbalah. Kabbalists state that there is no reality at all, but something called His Essence, the Upper Force.

As uncanny as it sounds, this notion hides in its wings the very prospect of freedom, for every person, for every nation, and for the entire world. The structure and the perception of reality are the surface of this book.

But the story of humanity, or more accurately, of the human soul, is the undercurrent that drives the reader forward in this book. It is about you; about me; about all of us. This book is about the way we were, the way we are, the way we will be, and most importantly, it is about the best way to get there.

The Science of Kabbalah: is the first in a series of texts that Rav Michael Laitman, Kabbalist and scientist, designed to introduce readers to the special language and terminology of the Kabbalah. Here, Rav Laitman reveals authentic Kabbalah in a manner that is both rational and mature. Readers are gradually led to an understanding of the logical design of the Universe and the life whose home it is.

The Science of Kabbalah, a revolutionary work that is unmatched in its clarity, depth, and appeal to the intellect, will enable readers to approach the more technical works of Baal HaSulam (Rav Yehuda Ashlag), such as *Talmud Eser Sefirot* and *Zohar*. Although scientists and philosophers will delight in its illumination, laymen will also enjoy the satisfying answers to the riddles of life that only authentic Kabbalah provides. Now, travel through the pages and prepare for an astonishing journey into the Upper Worlds.

Introduction to the Book of Zohar: is the second in a series written by Kabbalist and scientist Rav Michael Laitman, which will prepare readers to understand the hidden message of "*The Zohar*". Among the many helpful topics dealt with in this companion text to

The Science of Kabbalah, readers are introduced to the "language of roots and branches," without which the stories in *The Zohar* are mere fable and legend. Introduction to *The Book of Zohar* will certainly furnish readers with the necessary tools to understand authentic Kabbalah as it was originally meant to be, as a means to attain the Upper Worlds.

Wondrous Wisdom: This book presents the first steps, an initial course on Kabbalah, based solely on authentic teachings passed down from Kabbalist teacher to student over thousands of years. Offered within is a sequence of lessons revealing the nature of the wisdom and explaining the method of attaining it. For every person questioning "Who am I really?" and "Why am I on this planet?" this book is an absolute must.

A Guide to the Hidden Wisdom of Kabbalah (with ten complete Kabbalah lessons): provides the reader with a solid foundation for understanding the role of Kabbalah in our world. The content was designed to allow individuals all over the world to begin traversing the initial stages of spiritual ascent toward the apprehension of the upper realms.

Kabbalah for Beginners: By reading this book you will be able to take your first step in understanding the roots of human behaviour and the laws of nature. The contents present the essential principals of the Kabbalistic approach and describe the wisdom of Kabbalah and the way it works. *Kabbalah for Beginners* is intended for those searching for a sensible and reliable method of studying the phenomenon of this world for those seeking to understand the reason for suffering and pleasure, for those seeking answers to the major questions in life. Kabbalah is an accurate method to investigate and define man's position in the universe.

The wisdom of Kabbalah tells us why man exists, why he is born, why he lives, what the purpose of his life is, where he comes from, and where he is going after he completes his life in this world.

ABOUT BNEI BARUCH

Bnei Baruch is a non-profit organization that is spreading the wisdom of Kabbalah to accelerate the spirituality of humankind. Kabbalist Rav Michael Laitman, PhD, who was the disciple and personal assistant to Rabbi Baruch Ashlag, the son of Rabbi Yehuda Ashlag (author of *The Sulam* commentary on *The Zohar*), follows in the footsteps of his mentor in leading the group toward its mission.

Laitman's scientific method provides individuals of all faiths, religions, and cultures with the precise tools necessary for embarking on a captivating path of self-discovery and spiritual ascent. With the focus being primarily on inner processes that individuals undergo at their own pace, Bnei Baruch welcomes people of all ages and lifestyles to engage in this rewarding process.

In recent years, a massive worldwide search for the answers to life's questions has been underway. Society has lost its ability to see reality for what it is and in its place superficial and often misleading concepts have appeared. Bnei Baruch reaches out to all those who are seeking awareness beyond the standard, people who are seeking to understand our true purpose for being here.

Bnei Baruch offers practical guidance and a reliable method for understanding the world's phenomena. The authentic teaching method, devised by Rabbi Yehuda Ashlag, not only helps overcome the trials and tribulations of everyday life, but initiates a process in which individuals extend themselves beyond their present boundaries and limitations.

Rabbi Yehuda Ashlag left a study method for this generation, which essentially "trains" individuals to behave as if they have already achieved the perfection of the Upper Worlds while still here in our world. In the words of Rabbi Yehuda Ashlag, "This method is a practical way to attain the Upper World, the source of our existence, while still living in this world."

A Kabbalist is a researcher who studies his or her own nature using this proven, time-tested and accurate method. Through this method, one attains perfection and control over one's life, and realizes life's true goal. Just as a person cannot function properly in this world without having knowledge of it, the soul cannot function properly in the Upper World without knowledge of it. The wisdom of Kabbalah provides this knowledge.

HOW TO CONTACT BNEI BARUCH

Bnei Baruch
1057 Steeles Avenue West, Suite 532
Toronto, ON, M2R 3X1
Canada

E-mail: info@kabbalah.info

Web site: www.kabbalah.info

Toll free in Canada and USA:
1-866-LAITMAN
Fax: 1-905 886 9697